D1286981

A **Queen**

in search of a **King**

A Queen

A

in search of a

King

Go ahead and ask Him for a date

JOHN MARSHALL

DEDICATION

I dedicate this book to my two divine originals, made in Heaven, my granddaughters Briana (13 years old) and Destiny (5 years old). Hopefully they will employ the principles presented in this book and reap rich rewards for doing so.

I have made a pact with Briana. Her first date has to get permission from me before he can take her out. That gives me an opportunity to influence the direction of their date or at least remind them of the direction in which their date should proceed.

I look forward to writing A Queen Who Found Her King *and featuring both my granddaughters. I trust that you could also write the book and feature your daughters, granddaughters, and great granddaughters as well.*

TABLE OF CONTENTS

INTRODUCTION

You may be thinking, "What credentials do you have that qualify you to write authoritatively on this subject?" One is qualified if one will think correctly and thoroughly and be willing to acknowledge the results that one observes. If that does not encourage you to keep reading, let me share two items for your pacification.

One, God intended for practically all men and women to become married. That dictates that some form of socializing, i.e. dating, would be necessary to lead them to become married. God intended for dating and marriage to be within the normal grasp of every person. He never intended for them to constantly need the professional help of a psychologist in order to date and remain successfully married. Although the occasional need for a therapist may arise, this would be the exception, not the rule. Each individual, however, must think correctly and think thoroughly about substantive issues relative to nature and the manner of their relationship.

You have noticed that friendship and communication are significant elements for a quality marriage. How will two people become friends except if they communicate and get to know the heart of each other? Therefore dating in such a way as to learn the heart of your prospective spouse just makes sense.

Two, during my thirty-plus years of life coaching, I have learned a few things. Frequently I ask married couples how they met and what were the links that led to marriage. I have observed that seemingly healthy married couples started out as just "good friends." Their friendship led them into marriage. Therefore if two people could date in such a manner as to first become good friends, they will insure the health of their marriage.

This book, therefore, is not designed to highlight my professionalism but rather to highlight common sense practices. Do these common sense practices work? What evidence do I have that they work? You may say, "I will not try them unless I know they work." Did you know that what you tried in the past would work before you tried it? If it had worked, you probably would not be reading this book. There are never guarantees in regard to human behavior. There are only probabilities. The probability is high that what I propose to you in this book will work.

Several years ago while driving through Texas listening to the radio, I heard about a book entitled *I Kissed Dating Goodbye* by Joshua Harris. I rushed out and bought a copy. Trust me; the content was far more titillating than the title. This book started me thinking in the direction that led to writing this book.

I am writing this book primarily for single women because of the dating frustration that I sense in so many single women. As a single woman, do you expect to find a good husband? Are you really ready to receive a good man with whom you can spend the rest of your life? If you are not mentally and emotionally ready to receive a good man, do you think that God should place him in your path? Why should God present you with a good man if your mindset will prevent your relationship from being successful? How devastating would it be for the good man, you, and the honor of God?

Do not be discouraged. All is not lost. God is not through with you yet. Guidance from God will put you in a place to receive a good man and potential husband. You must, however, prepare yourself to become a good wife. Yes, the queen must prepare herself to receive her king! In Proverbs 31, King Solomon, the wisest of all men, writes the words of King Lemuel's mother describing for us the type of woman who makes a virtuous wife. Centuries later this wisdom still rings true.

> The words of King Lemuel, the oracle which his mother taught him:
>
> What, O my son?
>   And what, O son of my womb?
>   And what, O son of my vows?
>   Do not give your strength to women,
>   Or your ways to that which destroys kings.
>   It is not for kings, O Lemuel,
>   It is not for kings to drink wine,
>   Or for rulers to desire strong drink,
>   For they will drink and forget what is decreed,
>   And pervert the rights of all the afflicted.
>   Give strong drink to him who is perishing,
>   And wine to him whose life is bitter.
>   Let him drink and forget his poverty
>   And remember his trouble no more.
>   Open your mouth for the mute,
>   For the rights of all the unfortunate.
>   Open your mouth, judge righteously,
>   And defend the rights of the afflicted and needy.
>
> An excellent wife, who can find?
>   For her worth is far above jewels.
>   The heart of her husband trusts in her,
>   And he will have no lack of gain.
>   She does him good and not evil
>   All the days of her life.

She looks for wool and flax
And works with her hands in delight.
She is like merchant ships;
She brings her food from afar.
She rises also while it is still night
And gives food to her household
And portions to her maidens.
She considers a field and buys it;
From her earnings she plants a vineyard.
She girds herself with strength
And makes her arms strong.
She senses that her gain is good;
Her lamp does not go out at night.
She stretches out her hands to the distaff,
And her hands grasp the spindle.
She extends her hand to the poor,
And she stretches out her hands to the needy.
She is not afraid of the snow for her household,
For all her household are clothed with scarlet.
She makes coverings for herself;
Her clothing is fine linen and purple.
Her husband is known in the gates,
When he sits among the elders of the land.
She makes linen garments and sells them,
And supplies belts to the tradesmen.
Strength and dignity are her clothing,
And she smiles at the future.
She opens her mouth in wisdom,
And the teaching of kindness is on her tongue.
She looks well to the ways of her household,
And does not eat the bread of idleness.
Her children rise up and bless her;
Her husband also, and he praises her, saying:
"Many daughters have done nobly,
But you excel them all."
Charm is deceitful and beauty is vain,

But a woman who fears the Lord, she shall be praised.
Give her the product of her hands,
And let her works praise her in the gates (Proverbs 31:1-31).

Let us consider the wisdom of King Lemuel's mother. Did you notice the avenue through which this wisdom came? King Lemuel's mother did not teach these virtues to a woman but instead taught them to her son (see verse 1).

She posed the question, "Who is a good woman that can become a good wife?" Then she set out to answer it. The Proverbs 31 woman honored the trust of her husband adding value to him, her children, and all under her jurisdiction. She exercised economical astuteness and financial savvy. She leveraged her finances and gained an adequate return on her financial investments. This woman wasted none of her time in idleness, but rather she maximized her efforts so that she could give to the needy. Her internal beauty and strength demanded an appraisal and approval from her husband, her children, and all who heard of her.

Is this the kind of woman that sister-girl conversations esteem? If not, why not? How much of your happy-hour freedom would you trade to be in the position of the Proverbs 31 woman?

Even today men need and cherish these internal spiritual values and rightly so, for they meet God's design for the wife. Good men are looking for good women. Become a good woman and you will be discovered by a good man. Be a good woman and you will discover a good man.

For many years, I have been hearing an echoing chorus of complaints from women about the negligent commitment attitude of men. I feel their pain. It should not be this way. Therefore I offer a solution.

When a woman introduces a man as her fiancée, I usually ask, "When is the big date?" Most often, she sheepishly and sometimes embarrassingly says, "We do not have one yet." The man seems annoyed that marriage is even mentioned. When a man and a woman have been dating for years and do not have a wedding date set, usually there is no marriage in the making. Why is the woman anticipating marriage and the man is only anticipating another date? Better yet, how do we fasten this disconnect?

A far higher percentage of women desire to be married while a much lower percentage of men are migrating toward marriage. Should we just complain about this or should we try to remedy this?

It seems that a far higher percentage of women desire to be married while a much lower percentage of men are migrating toward marriage. I feel your pain. Why? Should we just complain about this or should we try to remedy this? Is there really a way to get men to commit to being married? Is there a non-manipulative way to get men to commit to marriage? Yes, I believe there is a healthy way to get men to commit to marriage. It is called healthily dating. Therefore I have attempted to help women to fashion the dating culture toward marriage.

This book is written for the women and men who dare to trust the wisdom of God enough to try Him. By trying Him, you test Him. When you test Him, you will discover His trustworthiness.

Part 1

THE PREPARATION TO BECOME A WOMAN

Chapter 1

A GOD–FASHIONED WOMAN

GOD IS THE creator and sustainer of the universe. His creative and administrative power is the essence of our being. God is the object of our faith. His being and His desires should be the center of our desires.

God determined, "It is not good for the man to be alone" (Genesis 2:18). God decided that a wife was the most suitable helper for Adam. Therefore God made Adam a wife. He took Adam's rib and fashioned a suitable helper for Adam. Before Eve became a wife, she was a God-fashioned woman from Adam's rib. Be a woman from God and you can be wife for man.

Are you a God-fashioned woman or are you a Hollywood-fashioned woman? The values of a Hollywood-fashioned woman, one who has been captivated by the glitz and glamour of Hollywood, are likely to conflict with God's values. Are you ready to become a wife for man? Are you willing to listen to the accounts of women from God so that you can be a wife for man? There lies much wisdom in the stories told by women of God.

Wisdom from the world of women

God created man in His own image (see Genesis 1:26). In this verse, the term *man* was not used to identify gender, but was used as a plural noun. When used as a plural noun, the term *man* includes both men and women (see verses 26-27).

God deputized both men and women as custodial stewards of His creation. Although the accomplishments of women have often been overshadowed by the feats of men, women have contributed significantly to the spiritual well-being of our world. Besides King Lemuel's mother, let us consider some other valuable women in the Bible and the contributions they made.

Consider the wisdom of Anna

In Luke 2:36-38 we learn of a woman named Anna. Although very little detail is given, we do know that she was a prophetess who lived in Jerusalem during the time of the birth of Jesus. The prophetess "foretold" and "forth-told" the message of God. To foretell is to predict something before it happens, but to forth tell is to apply the message of God to current issues.

Anna remained a virgin until she married. God blessed her with a husband for only seven years. After her husband died, she remained a widow until she was eighty-four years. Anna set an example of godly dedication. She never left the temple. There she fasted, prayed, and served night and day. Likely, there were no living quarters at the temple. At some point, she must have gone home. It must have been that in her heart she never left the temple. Anna declared that Jesus would bring redemption to the people. Her excitement about her Lord drove her to enthusiastically speak of Him to all those who were interested. What a woman after God's own heart.

Today what is the primary objective of women? Is today's woman knowledgeable about the word of God? Is today's woman willing to unashamedly speak of the goodness of God? Is today's woman willing to remain a virgin until married? Is today's woman so dedicated to the house of the Lord? Do you serve the Lord in your heart at all times?

Consider the wisdom of Mary, the mother of Jesus Christ

The angel Gabriel informed the virgin Mary that God had chosen her to give birth to Jesus (see Luke 1:26-34). No virgin had ever born a child. Therefore Mary questioned how this could be. Humans have come into the world through four different means. God brought forth: (1) Adam, without using a man or a woman, (2) us, using both a man and a woman, (3) Eve, by using a man but without a woman, and (4) Jesus, using a woman without a man.

In spite of the seemingly impossible, Mary believed what God said about her (see verses 35-38). She conditioned herself to say what the Word says. In fact Mary began to say what the Word said—that she would give birth to a son—even before it happened (see verses 46-48). What she said became a reality; she gave birth to Jesus. Her own words became a creative force within her.

Mary also surrounded herself with people who would say what the Word says. Mary visited Elizabeth, mother-to-be of John the Baptist (see verses 39-45). How did Elizabeth know Mary was going to give birth? She believed the word Mary heard and had spoken to her. What a woman after God's own heart.

Do you believe what God has said in spite of it seeming impossible? Have you conditioned yourself to say what the Word says? Have you surrounded yourself with people who will say what the Word says? How well do you think the majority of today's women are doing at this?

Jesus complimented Mary for prioritizing the provisions of the soul over the preparations for the body.

Consider the wisdom of Mary, the sister of Lazarus

Scenario number one: Jesus visited Mary and Martha's home (see Luke 10:38-42). During His visit, Mary sat and listened to the word of the Lord. Mary concerned herself with the provisions for the soul. What a woman after God's own heart.

Scenario number two: Jesus visited Mary and Martha's home. During His visit, Martha stood and looked after the work of the house. Martha concerned herself with the preparations for the body.

Jesus complimented Mary for prioritizing the provisions of the soul over the preparations for the body. When you prioritize the provisions for the soul over the preparations for the body, God elevates your life to a higher level. He does this because He appreciates you for prioritizing what is essential. God compliments you for placing the one "good" thing above the many "going" things. Mary had chosen the one necessary "good" part while Martha chose to worry about the many necessary on-going preparations.

God lifts your life to a higher level because He appreciates you for prioritizing that which is eternal. God compliments you for placing the one permanent thing above the many personal things. Mary chose to listen to the eternal Word while Martha chose to look after the earthly work. When you prioritize the provisions for the soul over the preparations for the body, God lifts your life to a higher level. When God appreciates your choices, He appropriates His resources.

Questions

☐ What are your three most urgent agenda items for today and tomorrow?

1. _____

_____

2. _____

_____

3. _____

_____

☐ What difference will it make if you accomplish them or not?

_____

_____

_____

☐ How many of your urgent agenda items are provisions for the soul?

_____

_____

_____

☐ How many of your urgent agenda items are preparations for the body?

_____

_____

_____

Consider the wisdom of Pilate's wife

Pilate's wife was the only person, man or woman, who stood up for Jesus during His critical hour (see Matthew 27:19-26). She declared His innocence and forbade her husband from participating in the evil scheme designed by His adversaries. Although she agonized over the circumstances, Pilate's wife exercised the courage to interrupt her husband while he was making the most important decision of his life. Since she recognized that Jesus was a just and righteous man, she advised her husband correctly. The advice she gave her husband was contrary to that which he received from his close male associates, for none of them exercised restraints.

Pilate's wife was an example of godly interruption. Believing that Jesus was innocent, she interrupted her husband while he conducted official business. She interrupted to provide him with sage advice. Unfortunately her interruption did not yield her desired results. Pilate went ahead with the request of the audience and surrendered Jesus to be crucified. All good examples do not yield the desired results; nevertheless God really wants you to set examples as a godly woman. He wants all of us to follow the examples of godly women. What a woman after God's own heart.

Consider the wisdom of Jochebed

Jochebed was the wife of Amram, the mother of Moses, and a descendant of Levi. She set an example of godly expectation (see Exodus 2:1-10, 6:20). Pharaoh decided to kill all the Hebrew male babies (see Exodus 1:12-22). He ordered the midwives to destroy all male children at birth, but the midwives feared God so they were unafraid of Pharaoh. Defiantly they refused to honor Pharoah's ruthless command. Pharaoh then commanded his people to throw every Hebrew son into the Nile River.

Jochebed gave birth to Moses. By faith she hid him for three months (see Exodus 2:1-4). Faithfully she expected God to somehow rescue her son from the wrath of Pharaoh. She crafted a flotation pillow, placed Moses on it, and set it afloat in the Nile River. Moses' sister, Miriam, stood by expecting to see what would happen. Pharaoh's daughter saw the baby and rescued him from the Nile. When Miriam saw what happened, she asked Pharaoh's daughter if she would like for her to call a nurse for the baby. She consented and Miriam called her own mother so she could nurse Moses. What an awesome demonstration of the providence of God.

Because Jochebed fearlessly expected God to rescue her son from the wrath of Pharaoh (see Hebrews 11:23), she instilled faith in the next generation; her daughter, Miriam, stood by expecting to see what would happen after placing her brother in the Nile River in a basket. What a woman after God's own heart.

Questions

☐ Why do you think the king feared Hebrew sons more than he feared Hebrew daughters?

_____

_____

_____

_____

☐ How did the midwives respond? Why did they respond that way? What does that say about female connectedness to children?

_____

_____

_____

_____

☐ To what extent is that trait evident in today's society?

_____

_____

_____

_____

☐ To what extent is that trait absent in today's society?

_____

_____

_____

_____

☐ How can the female connectedness to their children be improved upon?

_____

_____

_____

_____

☐   What did God do for the midwives as a result of their allegiance to Him?

_____

_____

_____

_____

☐   Describe a time when you were defiant for God?

_____

_____

_____

☐   What was God's response to you?

_____

_____

_____

_____

Consider the wisdom of Abigail

Abigail was the wife of Nabal (see 1 Samuel chapter 25). She set an example of godly intervention. She intervened to minimize the evil that her husband had done. What a woman after God's own heart. Her husband, Nabal, was wealthy but worthless and he dealt cruelly with others. Because of his foolheartedness he did not help to make peace, so Abigail worked behind the scenes to preserve the peace between King David and Nabal.

While Nabal's shepherds cared for the king's sheep, King David treated them very kindly and asked a favor of Nabal. Nabal, however, refused to honor the king's request, so King David became enraged and set out to destroy Nabal. Abigail heard of David's anger and appeased him. She intervened to minimize the evil that her future husband, King David, would have done.

Women, you must rise to the occasion even when you have to go at it alone. When God is with you, you and He are always a majority. God really wants you to set examples as godly women.

Questions

☐   Read 1 Samuel 25:1-42. What do you think about Abigail?

_____

_____

_____

_____

☐ Do you think that Nabal married Abigail because of her external beauty or her internal beauty? Why? Why not?

_____

_____

_____

_____

☐ How likely had Abigail been an opportunist, exposing her beauty in order to attract a wealthy husband? Does the text indicate that in any way?

_____

_____

_____

_____

☐ When Nabal refused to help David's servants, to what extent was that refusal legitimate?

_____

_____

_____

_____

☐ Should Abigail have talked to her husband before she went to appease David, or should she have gone behind his back as she did? Why? Why not?

_____

_____

_____

_____

☐ Was she being disrespectful when she said her husband was worthless? To what extent may she have been using her glamour status to secure the favor of David?

_____

_____

_____

_____

☐ What evidence indicates that her approach had the favor of God? Is there any evidence that she did not have the favor of God?

_____

_____

_____

_____

☐ When and to what extent should a wife provide a favor for another man when her husband does not want to provide a favor for him?

_____

_____

_____

_____

☐ Contrast and compare Abigail's behavior with that of a submissive wife.

_____

_____

_____

_____

☐ What must it have been like to be married to a worthless but wealthy fool?

_____

_____

_____

_____

Consider the wisdom of the Shunammite woman

The Shunammite woman consulted with her husband about providing a resting place for the prophet Elisha (see 2 Kings 4:1-37). By providing comfortable and convenient lodging, the Shunammite woman blessed the prophet Elisha. Elisha blessed the Shunammite woman with the capacity to conceive a son. Her spoken words activated her blessing for Elisha and his blessing for her. In spite of her being very hospitable to the man of God, she experienced a great heartache because her son died. Later her heartache returned to happiness because Elisha brought her son back to life through the power of God. She spoke a word of faith in the midst of her grief and her heartache turned into happiness (see verses 21-26, Hebrews 11:35, 1 Kings 17:23).

Although her son was dead, she said, "It is well." What she said happened. What she said caused it to happen. Her spoken words programmed her life for life. Just as it was for the Shunammite woman, your faith-filled spoken words program your life for life. Faith-filled spoken words add value to the lives of those who know you. The Shunammite woman's faith-filled spoken words added value to the life of her son and to the life of her husband. Faith-filled spoken words add value to the lives of those who hear of them. Her faith-filled words added value to the life of those of her generation and subsequent generations (see Romans 15:4, Hebrews 11:4). Observe:

1. Life and hope do not have to be over until God says it is over.

2. Sometimes God says it is over only because we say it is over (see Genesis 18:32-33).

3. Things of value are obtained by sacrifice.

4. Things of value are maintained by sacrifice.

The Shunammite woman teaches us to speak hopefully until God has absolutely written the final sentence. What a woman after God's own heart.

Chapter 2

EMOTIONAL BRUISES

Y EARS AGO I counseled Randy and Shelia[1], an intelligent, college-educated, married couple. They came to me in the hope that I could help them through an explosion that had taken place in their marriage. Their marital conflict was still brewing on the Monday afternoon we met. They rode to our session in separate automobiles, sat in my office with their backs to each other, refused to acknowledge each other's presence, and spoke of each other in third-person plural—"they and them." As we explored their situation here is what we discovered.

Shelia's dilemma: Randy had a habit of "shooting" used cotton swabs toward the wastebasket. He often missed his target and the cotton swab landed on the floor. Whenever he missed the wastebasket, he would allow the cotton swab to remain on the floor for several days. Sometimes they would accumulate before he retrieved them and placed them in the wastebasket. During our session, Shelia reminded him that five cotton swabs were still lying on the floor.

The previous weekend, Randy and Shelia had planned to attend church on Sunday, go to brunch, go shopping, and attend an afternoon movie. Unfortunately on Saturday evening Randy again missed the wastebasket with his tossed cotton swab. An argument ensued and they spent the rest of the evening in silence, in separate rooms of the house. When they finally retired to bed, Randy attempted to initiate sexual intimacy but Shelia refused.

Sunday morning, Randy refused to get out of bed and get dressed for church. Shelia dressed and went to church alone. After church, she endured brunch alone before returning home. When she finally arrived home, Randy reminded her of their Sunday afternoon plans. Shelia informed him that she was uninterested in keeping their previously made plans. They had had no further communication with each other until they arrived for their coaching session with me.

Randy's dilemma: Shelia had a habit of coming out of the bathroom and into the bedroom while flossing her teeth. This flossing of teeth in the bedroom infuriated Randy and he regularly complained about it. During our session he lamented, "She keeps flicking her germs out into the air in the bedroom, when she should do that in the bathroom."

Upon further discussion, I discovered the bruised emotional context in which Shelia had lived. She had been raised in a house with a mother and father who seemed to truly love her and each other. However her parents were traditional in that her father made the decisions for the family and his wife obediently honored them. Shelia felt that her father's stern manner intimidated her mother. Although her mother never complained, Shelia thought her father took unfair advantage of her mother. At an early age, she decided that she would not allow her own husband to "walk on her." She made up her mind to stand toe-to-toe with every man and make sure that no man got the upper hand. Therefore when Randy took advantage of her by disrespecting her clean house, she saw vestiges of her father and felt a need to sternly straighten him out.

Upon further discussion, I discovered the bruised emotional context in which Randy had also lived. His mother was a neat freak.

Everything in the house had to remain neatly placed in its properly assigned space. Randy and his father were never able to escape his mother's complaining wrath. His mother was always yelling and telling them what and what not to do. So years later when Shelia complained, Randy saw vestiges of his mother and experienced painful emotional flashbacks. He decided that he would not spend the rest of his life running to pick up a cotton swab just because Shelia demanded it.

The situation had now moved beyond cotton swabs and dental floss, and the marriage relationship was in jeopardy. How does missing the wastebasket with five cotton swabs and flossing one's teeth in the bedroom create such marital chaos? It doesn't, unless there is a bruised emotional context just waiting beneath the surface. To preserve marital harmony, Randy probably should have honored his wife's request and immediately retrieved his cotton swabs and placed them in the wastebasket when he missed his goal. However five cotton swabs lying on the floor should have been harmless. To preserve marital harmony, Shelia probably should have honored her husband's request and finished her flossing in the bathroom. However germs were already being transferred by kisses between the couple. Shelia's flossing in the bedroom should have been harmless.

Shelia had a right to expect Randy to honor her wishes. Randy had a right to expect Shelia to honor his wishes. However for the sake of the relationship, neither should have allowed their unfilled expectations to threaten their marital relationship. Why did these seemingly small issues rise to the level of being relationship-threatening issues? Past emotional bruises made each of them overly sensitive to each other's behavior.

Emotional bruises: a major hazard along the path of preparation

An emotional bruise is a mental cut or stab into one's self-esteem, self-concept, and/or personal identity.

Many women suffer from emotional bruises. An emotional bruise is a mental cut or stab into one's self-esteem, self-concept, and/or personal identity. Emotional bruises come from real or imagined blows to one's personal identity. These blows usually come from an authority figure and may even stem from a misperception of the authority figure. For example, Satan made Eve believe that God unfairly withheld something good from her when he said, "For God knows that in the day you eat from it [the tree] your eyes will be opened, and you will be like God, knowing good and evil" (Genesis 3:5). However Eve was already like God, for she had been created in His image. In Genesis 1:27 we are told, "God created man in His own image, in the image of God He created him; male and female He created them." Eve suffered from the deception of perception.

Deception of perception takes place when one's perception is untrue. That untruth deceives one into believing a lie. Therefore the individual is deceived by his own perception. Eve perceived that Satan was a person of authority and she was misguided by his information. Satan's misinformation caused Eve to respond detrimentally to her own well-being.

When one internalizes the actions of another in such a way that they demean and demote self-esteem, self-concept, and/or personal identity, a bruise occurs. For example, Robert[2], a member of the church where I was the minister, had suffered a severe emotional bruise in grade school. When he was in the sixth grade, his math teach ordered him to the blackboard to solve a mathematical equation. He did not solve the problem correctly and the teacher embarrassed him in front of the entire class. Although this happened forty-five years ago, to this day he becomes paranoid in front of an audience. Without knowing his history, I assigned Robert to serve as one of the collectors of the Sunday morning contribution. He immediately quit attending the assembly and remained absent for six months. Eventually he came by the office and told me why he left, his history, and made me promise never again to assign him a job where he would be in front of an audience. Indeed, Robert had suffered a severe emotional bruise from which he never healed.

When a female suffers an emotional bruise she is much like an apple. If you drop an apple on a hard surface it will bruise. The bruise does not become noticeable immediately, but eventually appears in a few hours. Wait a few days, and the apple becomes rotten. In women the bruise may not show up immediately, but there is a bruise spot in her personality that will eventually show up. She may think that an emotional bruise will just go away in time, but instead it gets worse and negatively impacts her emotional, social, and intimate relationships.

She may think that an emotional bruise will just go away in time, but instead it gets worse and negatively impacts her emotional, social, and intimate relationships.

Many men and women suffered emotional bruises during their childhood. Some wounds were caused by the presence of a dysfunctional mother and/or father. Some wounds were caused by the absence of a functional father and/or mother. In either case, far too often children carry their emotional bruises into adulthood. Then while dating the male and female begin to massage and scratch each other's bruises. Their interactions produce cancerous sores that sabotage healthy dating relationships. When they ignore the obvious warning signals and persist into marriage, the cancerous sores continue to erupt.

Many women suffered emotional bruises during childhood. In fact some women believe that early interactions with their fathers or brothers have negatively affected the way they relate to men in their adulthood. Consequently these women believe that since they were bruised by men in their childhoods, they will inevitably be bruised by their boyfriends and/or husbands.

Unfortunately emotional bruising is a perpetual cycle. More often than not, bruised individuals unintentionally inflict emotional bruises on others. Bruised men will bruise the women in their lives and vice versa. Exactly how does this happen? Here is the cycle: (1) Unhealthy critique leads to unhealthy competition. (2) Unhealthy competition leads to unhealthy resistance. (3) Unhealthy resistance leads to unhealthy resentment. (4) Unhealthy resentment leads to unhealthy rebellion. (5) Unhealthy rebellion leads to unhealthy removal. (6) An unhealthy removal leads to an unhealthy replacement. (7) Unhealthy replacement starts the cycle all over again. Here are common examples of the bruising cycle.

A daughter may become emotionally bruised by her father.

A daughter may become emotionally bruised by her father's response, or her perception of his response, to her mother. She may come to believe that her father is overbearing toward her mother. She may assume her feminine identity with her mother and begin to emotionally absorb the blows placed upon or perceived to be placed upon her mother by her father. For example many children will cry when they see their mother being physical abused. They tend to connect emotionally with their mother and emotionally share in the pain or the perceived pain that their mother is experiencing. The same is true when children perceive their mother is being emotionally abused. They wear the emotional wounds of their mother. These can include:

> **Critique:** A daughter evaluates her father's relationship with her mother and concludes that he is unfair towards her mother's personal identity. In other words she feels the self-esteem attack that her mother experiences. She sees her mother being robbed of her personal need to be a self-determining person.

> **Competition:** She competes with her father for her mother's attention. She seeks to draw her mother away from her father's behavior.

> **Resistance:** She begins to deny her father's wisdom so that she can, without conscious conflict, disobey her father's instructions and ignore his influence.

> **Resentment:** She feels insulted not only by her father's behavior but also by the fact that he doesn't know better.

She may even resent her mother for tolerating this abuse. She becomes displeased to the point of becoming indignant toward her father. A negative attitude surfaces, which she is unavailable to overcome. I purposely chose the word *unavailable* rather than *unable*. To be unable is to not have the wherewithal to overcome, thus becoming a permanent victim. She is unavailable, meaning she has not utilized the internal strength and cooperating strategies she has that would enable her to overcome.

Rebellion: Now she verbally confronts her father. This confrontation creates a negative resentment, which she is unavailable to overcome.

Removal: She now stays away from home. She goes out of her way to stay away from her father, even rebelling in order to avoid his presence.

Replacement: In spite of her emotional bruises, she longs to fill the father-shaped hole in her soul. The father-shaped hole is the emotional space designed by the Creator in which the essence of her father should be placed. She unwisely replaces her father with her boyfriend. This seems to work for a while, but only because her boyfriend's behavior has not yet reminded her of her father's behavior toward her mother. Likely her boyfriend treats her nicely and she wishes her father would treat her mother just as nicely. This seems to work for a while, but only because her boyfriend is not bruising her mother's identity.

Emotionally bruised by an ex-husband, former boyfriend, or casual dating acquaintance

We can find the same pattern of emotional wounds in this scenario:

Critique: Have you ever noticed two people who argue all the time? If one says something is good, the other says it is bad. They appear to have a "just-can't-get-along" attitude. Critique starts early and is often disguised as comedy or even casual conversation.

Competition: Girlfriend/wife seems to get satisfaction out of one-upping her boyfriend/husband. There is a constant string of score keeping. All winnings, however insignificant, are loudly announced.

Resistance: Girlfriend/wife has an "I-can-never-give-in-or-allow-you-to-enjoy-a-victory" attitude. Even when she has been outmatched, she makes an excuse to avoid giving just due.

Resentment: Girlfriend/wife develops an "I-can't-stand-you" attitude. However subtle initially, eventually it will become evident.

Rebellion: The couple becomes unwilling to relate comfortably toward each other in social settings.

Removal: A cessation of social interaction and a search to remove self from the physical presence of the other person.

Replacement: She replaces this man with another one. She has high hopes that this relationship will be better than the last. Too often it is not. Rather it is just more of the same.

Emotionally bruised women may become angry with God.

How many times have you heard women discuss the pain of going through their female physical issues? Even a routine physical exam for a woman is quite different than for a man. Have you noticed the frustration of women having to endure a menstrual cycle, hormone shifts, PMS, hot flashes, and the like? Why do women and not men have to endure this? The obvious answer is that God made them that way. Would you not be angry with One who relegated you to such pain but let the other gender roam pain free? What pain do men naturally have to endure?

How many times have you heard women discuss the biblical idea of submission? Did you hear them cursing under their breath about how some man wrote the Bible? Years ago while preaching a sermon that emphasized how Christ was the head and Savior of the church, I read the apostle Paul's statement, "Wives, be subject to your own husbands, as to the Lord. For the husband is the head of the wife, as Christ is also is the head of the church, He Himself being the Savior of the body" (Ephesians 5:22-23). When the service ended, one of the congregation members, Robin[3], stood waiting for me in the aisle with an angry scowl on her face. As I got close to her, she blurted out, "I need to talk to you."

We entered my office and I turned to hear what was on her mind. She sternly said, "You should never read those verses unless you are going to explain the husband and wife's roles." I reminded her that the sermon had not been about the family dynamic, but had been about Christ and the church. Therefore I asked why she felt that way. She informed me that her husband used (misused) this verse when he wanted to have sexual intercourse with her. He told her that to submit meant to have sexual intercourse. When he was interested in sexual gratification, he would say, "Submit to me." To make matters worse, he told her that I taught that concept in a men's Bible class. Never had I nor will I ever teach such dysfunctional theology.

Did you notice that she was angry with me because she thought I was the source of the ideology that brought about her abuse? Is it unreasonable to believe that some women are angry with God for they believe that if God is not fully to blame, He is at least partly to blame for their dilemma?

Likely some have become angry with God because they believe that the architect of the universe is guilty of design bias or flaw. They perceive that the system of God's design continues to unfairly penalize females. Often these women feel a need to bond together and attack every indicator of a masculine presence that they believe will promote God's unfairness.

Help for the emotionally bruised woman

Ultimately God is concerned with the whole person. He is concerned about the bruised person. He is concerned about you. One purpose of the coming of Jesus was to set free those who have been emotionally bruised. "The Spirit of the Lord is upon me, because He anointed me to preach the gospel to the poor. He has sent me to proclaim release to the captives, and recovery of sight to the blind, to set free those who are oppressed" (Luke 4:18). Note the phrase,

How you respond to your emotional bruising is significant.

"to set free those who are oppressed." The Greek word for *bruised* here is *thrauo* and it means "to be broken into pieces." If you are bruised, then you qualify! Jesus came to set you free from your bruised identity.

How do you know if you are emotionally bruised? Everyone has been emotionally bruised—but how you respond to your emotional bruising is significant. Analyze your response to unfulfilled expectations. Is the intensity of your response fully justified? If your boyfriend/husband forgets your birthday or an anniversary and you pour gasoline on his clothes and set them afire, the intensity of your response is not justified. Ask several objective friends to elaborate on the intensity of your responses to several situations. Do you have problems letting go of disappointments? Do you plot revengeful activities?

Jesus was emotionally bruised. Notice the cuts to His personal identity. The town in which He grew up, Nazareth, was considered a bad town (see John 1:46). When he was twelve, his parents misunderstood Him. They could not fully comprehend how He was the Son of God and must be about the business of His Father's house (see Luke 2:48-50). His friends once publicly accused Him of being "out of his mind" (Mark 3:21 NIV). Once when he spoke in the synagogue, his family and friends were highly offended by him (see Matthew 13:57-58). On at least one occasion, the spiritual leaders of His day publically accused Him of being demon possessed (see Matthew 12:24). The chief priests, scribes, and elders questioned His identity (see Mark 11:27-28). Because He claimed to be the Son of God, the Jewish leaders sought to kill Him (see John 5:18, 19:7). When things really got tough for Him, all His close friends deserted Him. One even denied knowing Him (see Matthew 26:24, 69-75).

He was sentenced to be crucified as a common criminal between two thieves (see Matthew 27:38).

How did Jesus overcome rejection? He found His identity in His heavenly Father (see Matthew 3:17, John 10:30). He didn't take offense at the actions of others (see John 5:19). He forgave those who bruised and rejected Him (see Luke 23:34). He even loved and blessed those who rejected Him (see Matthew 5:44, Luke 6:27-35). He looked forward to the victory in the end (see Hebrews 12:2).

How does He provide healing for your bruises? He provides you with a new identity. Through Jesus you become a child of God (see John 1:12, Romans 8:16). Jesus became a substitute for your emotional hurts (see Hebrews 4:15).

Since Jesus carries your emotional hurts there is no need for you to continue to carry your own emotional baggage. "Woman, thou art loosed!" (Luke 13:12 KJV). Praise the Lord, praise the Lord. Now you can identify your emotional bruises, let go of them, enjoy a functionally healthy dating relationship, and eventually a healthy marriage relationship. Thank God almighty, you are free at last.

Part 2

THE PRESENTATION
TO BECOME A WIFE

Chapter 3

DATING: A NECESSARY PHASE

TRACY MCMILLAN WROTE an article that appeared in the February 11, 2011, edition of the *Huffington Post*. In it she provided six reasons why women are not married, which I will paraphrase:

1. You are angry and scare dates away.

2. You are shallow and want a trophy.

3. You are sleazy and settle for a romp instead of a ring.

4. You are not honest; you want to marry but pretend you do not.

5. You are selfish and think mostly of yourself.

6. You are convinced you are not good enough.

Certainly you are at liberty to disagree with Ms. McMillan but before you do, compile you own list of six and test their validity. Could it be that the biggest reason women are not married is because their emotional bruises prevent them from getting there? Could it be that an emotional bruise lies in the background of several if not all of the six preceding reasons?

Regina Brett, a columnist at *The Plain Dealer* in Cleveland, Ohio, wrote an article in her February 20, 2011, column in which she said, "We send out energy in the world and attract what we send. For years I dated, but sent energy that said, 'Come here, go away.' After counseling to heal my bruises, I sent one clear message: I'm ready to love and be loved. Then I stopped looking and poof! Along came my husband."

Comedian Redd Foxx once joked about himself saying, "Only one thing kept me out of college: high school." Unfortunately for some, high school is a necessary "evil" on the path toward college. Although it is not funny, "Only one thing keeps many women away from matrimony: dating." Dating is that evasive phase on the path toward marriage.

The subtitle of this book is where we will now turn: "Go ahead and ask Him for a date." Yes, I have purposefully capitalized "Him." You are asking Him for a date as well as him—God as well as the man. You are asking God to guide your steps spiritually as you progress through the seven dates intellectually. You are asking the man for a "social" date. That is, you are asking him for a date as in going out on a date. And you are indirectly asking the man for a "chronological" date. During your successful dating sessions you will be moving toward a date for the wedding. Through healthily dating, even the man will desire to become married, propose, set the date, and delightfully stand at the altar with you.

Dating: What is it?

First, let's define dating. Dating, as I use it in this book, is the sifting process through which a woman gets to know the character and characteristics of a man, intending to become his wife. Dating is a sifting process not a sorting process. When you sort, you rank and keep all. When you sift, you eliminate all except the final one.

Ranking perceived-to-be-good men in your subconscious will provide confusing smoke that will regularly rise throughout your marriage. Far too often, even if only for a moment, you will wonder how life would have been if you had married another man from your past. Unfortunately to their detriment, far too many women use dating as a sorting process rather than a sifting process. Many of the men you meet should never be brought into your life. Some are good men but not good for you. Some are not good for you at this time. Others with their present disposition are not good for any woman at any time. Why waste your time? The mature woman does not ask, "Is it right or wrong to date him?" but rather, "Is it best for me to date him now?"

Before you start sifting, make two lists. List one should contain the maximum of all the character and characteristics that you would like to have in your husband. List two contains the minimum of character and characteristics that you must have in your husband. For example, if you absolutely positively will never marry a man who has three "baby mommas," why start dating him?

Before you critique him, make sure that you qualify on your own list. If you are not a woman of character, you will have difficulty identifying a man of character. Being a person of character will enable you to show grace and mercy toward those who are imperfect.

Before you begin making your lists, study God's approved character and characteristic list. Train yourself to see and value what God sees and values. What does God look for in a man? When He needed men to allocate daily resources to women, He chose men who had good reputations and were full of the spirit and wisdom (see Acts 6:3). Why would you choose any less? When God needed men to become example leaders within the church, once again He specified the character and characteristics (see 1 Timothy 3:1-7, Titus 1:5-9). For example, God wanted church leaders to:

1. Be patient (not unduly rigorous).

2. Be vigilant (abstain from contaminants that control one's passions and diminish alertness).

3. Be hospitable (fond of strangers and foreigners).

4. Have a good reputation from without (among non-members).

5. Be willing to teach.

6. Be the husband of one wife (a one-woman kind of man).

7. Not be a brawler (one who has already decided to harshly retaliate).

8. Not be given to wine.

9. Not be a striker (one who physically retaliates).

10. Not be greedy of filthy lucre (desirous of illegal or unethical gains).

11. Not be covetous (seek to unwholesomely obtain that which already belongs to someone else).

Make sure both lists contain spiritual character and characteristics. Obviously the man you are seeking may not have prior husband

and father experience. He should, however, have a husband and father perspective of life. Otherwise why would you place a husband to be your "head" without verifying that he has the capacity to be a great husband and father?

When you meet a guy who does not meet your minimum list, do not give him any digits, not even your zip code. Do not enroll in the university of rehabilitation and recuperation. Let him find a physician to heal him. A therapist for a wife becomes a constant nag. A patient for a husband becomes a constant drag.

Maximum character and characteristics of someone I would like to have as a husband	Minimum character and characteristics of someone I would like to have as a husband
1.	1.
2.	2.
3.	3.
4.	4.
5.	5.
6.	6.
7.	7.
8.	8.
9.	9.
10.	10.

When to start dating

Learn to enjoy reading a good book—one that stimulates your intellect toward solutions to problems. A good book is like a good date. You get a chance to spend time alone. Like a date, a good book can carry you to the pinnacle of emotional ecstasy and into the valley of despair.

Why shop if you are not going to buy? Why date if you can't or aren't ready to marry?

Many people have lunged into serious financial trouble by shopping when they were ill prepared to buy. Why shop if you are not going to buy? Why date if you can't or aren't ready to marry? Enjoy your singleness. The sustaining joy of good group friendships is far more fun than the agony of bad one-to-one relationships. The single life is a God-governed, gifted, and good life (see 1 Corinthians 7:1-9).

Think of dating as an intellectual exploration in search of a spouse. Do not think of dating as just a lifestyle. Remember, life is about what God wants not just what you want. Therefore occasionally you may have to avoid what feels good for what is good.

Start dating only within twenty-four months of the time when you would become married. If you start dating before you are ready to marry, what do you do when you meet your potential husband? If he is ready to marry you after twelve months of dating but you are not ready, what does he do? You say wait. This waiting may prove to be very destructive to your future marriage. He may resent having to wait. He may seek another. Remember, he is waiting without a commitment. You may resent being pressured. You, too, may seek another who is just willing to socialize. The intimate energy that the anticipation of becoming married creates may propel you beyond the spiritual boundaries that you have set. You may find yourself compromising. I believe one reason why Satan has created the category of "unmarried and committed" is to ease away the guilt feelings of cohabitation before marriage. When two people join the committed crowd it just seems natural for them to take their relationship to a new level that includes sexual intercourse. Now that they are committed and not just sleeping around, their guilt feelings are likely to be weaker.

Before you begin dating, conquer any impediments you feel you must overcome before you get married. For example, if you need to improve your credit score or pay off school loans, do so or at least have the end in sight before you begin dating. Before you begin dating, achieve the goals that you believe you must achieve before you become married. At least wait until you are within reach of those goals to start dating. For example, if you want to complete your education before you marry, then have a graduation date for that degree before you start dating. If you want to travel and see the world before becoming married, then visit several states and at least one foreign country before beginning to date. If you feel you must freely spend your money without any restrictions, travel to the Netherlands, or buy a red convertible BMW, do all those things before you start dating.

Now you will ask, "But why can I not enjoy dating while I accomplish those things?" We will address that question later when we discuss how the "third-party" entertainer hounds a date and haunts a marriage.

Chapter 4

DATING: THE WRONG WAY

U NFORTUNATELY DATING THE wrong way will bind you into an unravelable cord of emotional emptiness with a man of your past. Even after you have married and begun life anew with another man, the history of your past may haunt the subsequent relationship.

Due to improper dating habits, many unmarried women painfully wrestle with the breakup of a dating relationship. Far too often they never fully heal from the breakup. I have noticed that unmarried women tend to grieve more over a dating breakup than married women do over a divorce. How many divorced women do you know who desire to resume their marriage with the ex? Probably very few. Yet how many single women do you know who desire to resume their dating relationship with their ex? Probably more than a few.

With all things considered, I believe that unmarried women are more traumatized by a dating breakup than married women are by a divorce. Why? How did this happen? What is the problem?

Herein lies the problem. Four types of relationships exist; God authorizes only the first two, but Satan authorizes the additional two. The four categories are: (1) Unmarried and uncommitted,

Four types of relationships exist; God authorizes only the first two, but Satan authorizes the additional two.

(2) married and committed, (3) unmarried and committed, and (4) married and uncommitted.

For the unmarried, God does not authorize a social companionship that includes sexual intercourse. Sexual intercourse is exclusively for those who are married and the exclusivity of marriage. God approves of a man and a woman to be married and thus committed. For the married, God authorizes a social companionship that includes sexual intercourse. The wisdom of God reserves sexual intimacy for the marriage bond (see 1 Corinthians 7:1-5; Hebrews 13:4). He does not approve of the unmarried being committed to provide sexual intimacy.

Satan approves of and sanctions a man and a woman to be unmarried and committed to a social companionship that would include sexual intercourse. Also Satan approves of a man and a woman to be married and uncommitted to a social companionship that would include sexual intercourse (see 1 Corinthians 6:9, Hebrews 13:4).

In other words, God leads you toward the *sacrifice* while Satan just leads you toward the *sack*. Even Christians have been swept away into these demonically driven third and fourth categories. Unmarried believers unashamedly declare that they are in a committed relationship and married believers declare their availability. Isn't it strange that many who are married are trying to get out of being committed and those who are unmarried are trying to become committed?

Years ago mothers and also especially grandmothers would say to single women, "Honey child, don't you be in love with him more than he is in love with you." That was their way of saying, "Do not be committed to him while he is uncommitted to you." For him to be committed to you is to become married to you. Otherwise you are a disaster waiting to happen.

I have heard many objections to God's plan, the most popular being, "Married people breakup. They marry and do not keep their commitment. So what is the difference?" Herein lies the difference. When you are married and committed, God seeks to preserve that relationship while Satan seeks to destroy it. When you are unmarried and committed, God seeks to destroy that relationship while Satan seeks to preserve it. The paramount questions are these: "Who would you prefer to be helping you, God or Satan? Who would you prefer to work against, God or Satan?"

You may ask these questions: "How do two people get to know each other unless they become committed? Can they come to really know each other without being in a committed relationship? Should not two people become committed for a while to see if this is what they really want to do?" These are all valid questions. We will seek God's answers to them.

Is there ever an instance wherein God recommends living together as husband and wife to see if you want to become husband and wife?

Did God provide an opportunity for Adam and Eve to live together before they became married? Is there ever an instance wherein God recommends living together as husband and wife to see if you want to become husband and wife? The answer to both questions is no.

Michael McManus in his book *Marriage Savers* provides these startling statistics:

- More than eight out of ten couples who live together will break up either before the wedding or afterward in divorce.

- About forty-five percent of those who begin cohabiting do not marry. Another five-to-ten percent continue living together and do not marry.

- Couples who do marry after living together are fifty percent more likely to divorce than those who did not.

- Only twelve percent of couples who have begun their relationship with cohabitation end up with a marriage lasting ten years or more.

God in His book The Holy Bible provides these startling statements:

"There is a way which seems right to a man, but its end is the way of death" (Proverbs 14:12). This scripture stands against the arguments, "Everyone is doing it. It's the new way. It's accepted in society." That may all be true, but just because a path seems right doesn't make it so.

"There is an appointed time for everything…a time to embrace and a time to shun embracing" (Ecclesiastes 3:1, 5).

"For this is the will of God, your sanctification; that is, that you abstain from sexual immorality; that each of you know how to possess his own vessel in sanctification and honor, not in lustful passion, like the Gentiles who do not know God" (1 Thessalonians 4:3-5).

"Marriage is to be held in honor among all, and the marriage bed is to be undefiled; for fornicators and adulterers God will judge" (Hebrews 13:4).

The marriage bed can be kept pure only when the sexual relationship is kept within marriage. Anything else brings God's judgment. Do you love your partner? Then why would you invite God's judgment into his life? Why would you willfully rob him of God's blessing?

My observations tend to suggest that the ending of an uncommitted relationship often causes more problems than the ending of a committed relationship. Investing too much time in trying to get a commitment proves to be too expensive. How can you avoid this type of problem? Date the biblical way. Guard and protect your emotions with your intellect. In the absence of undue emotional sensationalism, you will make better choices. Therefore you should date intellectually first and then emotionally. Reserve sexual intimacy until marriage. Do not start engaging in behavior that will ignite your passions and send hormones surging that you cannot control.

Your emotional investment will lead you to waste too much time dating a man who will never marry you or one that you should never marry. The stress of prolonged emotional investment burns itself into an emotional bruise. Emotional bruises grow into emotional scars—bruises that grow larger and affect more of one's life's decisions. Emotional scars become cancerous, even after you have moved into marriage with another man. Emotional scars sabotage your marriage and perpetually suck the joy out of your marriage.

In his book *I Kissed Dating Goodbye*[4], Joshua Harris tells a story from the masculine side. Allow me to tell it from the feminine side:

"It was finally here—David's wedding day, the day he had dreamed about and planned for years. As Henrietta walked down the aisle toward David, his heart surged within him. He gently took her hand and they turned toward the altar. But as the minister began to lead them through their vows, an unthinkable thing happened. A man stood up and quietly walked to the altar and took Henrietta's other hand. Another man stood up walked down the aisle and stood next to the first man. Then another man stood up and took his place beside the second man. Soon a chain of seven men stood by her as she repeated her vows to David.

David whispered to Henrietta, "Is this some kind of joke? Who are these men?"

"These are men of my past sexual experiences," she replied. "But they do not mean anything to me now...but I did give part of my heart to each of them."

With tears rolling down his cheeks, David said, "I thought your heart was all mine."

"It is," she pleaded. "Everything that is left is yours."

Many husbands pay the price for emotional baggage and bruises they did not create. The soul-singing O'Jays said it this way: "Your body's here with me, but your mind is on the other side of town. You're messing me around."

Dating the proper way is the key to making sure this does not happen. Through dating two people can come to know each other adequately. But what is dating? Is it not being in a committed relationship?

Chapter 5

DATING: WHO IS REALLY ENTERTAINING?

D URING THE TYPICAL date there is usually a third-party enter-tainer. For example, boy picks up girl in a shiny new car that has provided curb appeal. While they are riding in the car to the theater, Luther (Vandross) entertains her on the radio. At the theater, Denzel (Washington) entertains her on the screen. Later at the restaurant, Benihana (the chef) entertains her on the plate. When they attend a sporting event King James (LeBron) entertains her on the basketball court. Consequently after months of rotating through this vicious cycle, the dating couple has only engaged in surface and superficial conversation. They neither know anything of substance about each other nor do they know how to extract substance from one another.

Unfortunately far too many individuals date at this superficial level. The dating is all about making concessions to impress the other person. Concessions are made that will definitely cease after "I do" has been said. During the dating phase, couples date on a superficial level. They treat each other nicer and interpret each other's treatment to be nicer than they likely will after they become married. During pre-marriage preparation sessions, I inform couples that because they have dated on a superficial level, once they are married their negatives go up and their positives go down. When marriage happens, reality sets in. They interpret each other and each other's actions differently. A portion of this change is real but a portion of this change is perceived. Regular interaction and the close proximity of the two tend to test toleration limits.

For instance when I was a child my parents etched into my mind not to eat and drink everything that someone offered to me. While I was at the community store with my father, two brothers from the community, Lenzie and Arthur, stopped by to purchase sodas for their dates. Lenzie purchased a Coke and returned to his car to give it to his waiting date. She rejected the soda and reminded him that she wanted a Pepsi. He returned to the store and offered me the Coke. Because of my home training, I refused to accept the drink. To assure me the Coke was all right for me to drink, he informed me that he had misunderstood his date's request and purchased a Coke instead of a Pepsi.

I have often wondered what would have happened had they already been married. Would he have been so conciliatory? Should he have been so conciliatory? You and I both know that these acts of kindness are far too often relegated to the dating phase of a relationship and do not carry over into marriage.

Often times you do not marry the man that you date. You are not the woman you were when you were dating. Marriage produces a noticeable transformation. During thirty years of pastoring and counseling I have noticed how a seemingly passive woman dates an aggressive man. During this period of time, she surrenders to most of his preferences, even the ones that conflict with her ethical code. Once the wedding date is set, she begins to migrate toward her preferences. By the day of the wedding, it seems, she is now ready to stand on all her ground. Therefore the day after the wedding, she is quite different. Her husband is stunned to discover the stranger in the house and bed with him after the wedding.

This shock comes because many of the emotional bruises that occurred before the wedding or that were even caused by someone else have now surfaced to plague the wife and sabotage the marriage. Emotional bruises created before the marriage may become more noticeable after the marriage.

Here is another example. Let me tell you about Genevieve[5]. At the age of sixteen, Genevieve experienced her first sexual intercourse as the result of a date rape. Unfortunately through that encounter, she also became pregnant. It is not unbelievable that during more than thirty years of marriage she has never been able to emotionally and intimately nurture her husband. As a matter of fact, they had been married almost twenty years before she even shared with her husband about the rape and the trauma she experienced.

Very frequently when coaching couples wherein the female has become sexually uninterested or is failing to achieve an orgasm, I have discovered that unresolved emotional resentment toward the father was often the root of the problem. Can you imagine how a marriage suffers when the wife is sexually unfulfilled? How uninterested in sexual intercourse will a wife become when she no longer achieves an orgasm? How disruptive to the marriage will a constant non-engaging or a negligibly engaging interest in sexual intercourse be?

Emotional bruises toward your father may lie dormant and surface only after your husband acts like your father (plays

Emotional bruises toward your father may lie dormant and surface only after your husband acts like your father.

the rank card), or is perceived to be acting like you perceived your father. The first time your husband plays the rank card, you transfer to your husband the unresolved resentment that you have held toward your father. For example, if while you were in junior high school, your father painted the house an ugly green color without consulting your mother and your friends made fun of your house for months, you would be somewhat embarrassed. You resented your father for making that decision without considering the wishes of the family. Now you are married. Your husband, without having discussed with you, brings home the green Pinto that he has purchased for you to drive. You are now likely to transfer the residual resentment for your father to your husband.

Emotional bruises resulting from your relationship with a former boyfriend may lie dormant and surface only after your marriage. Your heart may still host favor or disfavor toward him. In either case it could plague your marriage. Favorable feeling may still exist even toward a former abusive boyfriend, similar to the effect of the Stockholm Syndrome. The Stockholm Syndrome describes the behavior of kidnap victims who over time become sympathetic to their captors. The name derives from a 1973 hostage incident in Stockholm, Sweden. At the end of six days of captivity in a bank, several kidnap victims actually resisted rescue attempts and afterward refused to testify against their captors. Some have suggested that Elizabeth Smart and Patty Hearst were victims of Stockholm Syndrome.

If you feel you must, exercise your liberty and disagree with all my observed assumptions, but you cannot deny that for quite some time men and women have been engaged in an adversarial relationship. If nothing is said, then nothing will be done. My goal is to get the discussion on the table. Then others can diagnose and offer viable prescriptions. Now let the discussion proceed.

Dating: Initiating the date

The wise man, King Solomon, declared, "He who finds a wife finds a good thing and obtains favor from the Lord" (Proverbs 18:22). Many interpret this verse to mean that the woman must not be active in the pursuit of matrimony. They believe that women are to shuffle through life waiting for a man to call. If no man calls, they are to patiently submit to singleness. I do not believe that is what Solomon had in mind at all. I think he used the word *find* as in "discover." And even if the woman is to be discovered, she must position herself to be discovered. Therefore it is all right for a woman to be an initiator.

Now that you are a prepared woman you are ready to be presented as a wife. Consider the first marriage. When God had finished fashioning Eve into a woman, He presented her to Adam to become his wife "and brought her to the man" (Genesis 2:22). The woman came into the presence of the man. The woman moved toward the man. The woman was presented to the man. Her presentation caused the man to examine and recognize who she was. Adam declared, "She is now bone of my bones, and flesh of my flesh" (Genesis 2:23). He discovered their connectedness.

When you discover a man whom you believe is an unmarried, spiritually compassionate, progressive thinker, you may ask him out on a date. Say to him, "You seem to be an unmarried, spiritually compassionate, progressive thinker. If you are unmarried, I would like to get to know you better." If he responds in the affirmative, just ask, "Can we talk?"

Eve came into Adam's environment and he discovered their kinship. She came into his environment and he discovered their connectedness. Within this context for matrimony there lies unnoticed the context of intellectual discovery. Therefore before the wedding a man and a woman need to connect intellectually. Far too often dating is only about an attempt to connect emotionally so that they can hook up sexually.

Far too often dating is only about an attempt to connect emotionally so that they can hook up sexually.

Dating that heals emotional bruises

After becoming the right date, you must then date the right way. What does the word of God say about dating? The word of God emphasizes a pertinent principle that should govern your dating. Read the text of this scripture carefully so that you can grasp it. "Do not sharply rebuke an older man, but rather appeal to him as a father, to the younger men as brothers, the older women as mothers, and the younger women as sisters, in all purity" (1 Timothy 5:1-2).

God wants young men to treat older women in all purity, just as they would their biological mothers. He wants younger men to treat younger women in all purity, just as they would treat their biological sisters. If you are an older woman, you must not only expect to be but appreciate being treated as a mother in all purity. If you are a younger woman, you too must not only expect to be but appreciate being treated as a sister in all purity. Therefore as you date, think and do what you would think and do with your brother. Would you dress provocatively to go to the movie with your brother?

Now let the opposition begin. Before you oppose the wisdom of this advice, answer just one question: Does God know best? If He knows best, then you really should register no opposition. For the benefit of the obstinate ones, however, I will proceed and share more.

One way to avoid the emotional bruising that occurs during the dating phase is to have arranged marriages. Who will choose this path? Before you criticize prearranged marriages, consider their success rate. Frequently it is reported that prearranged marriages have only a seven percent divorce rate. I will admit that likely there are factors other than just the absence of the dating phase that contribute to the stability of these marriages. The view of marriage, commitment to marriage, and even tolerance are likely contributing factors. Should not these also be factors in the marriages that are contracted through dating?

A second way to avoid the emotional bruising that takes place during the dating phase is to date in a manner that heals the emotional bruises. It is to this area that we now proceed. I will outline the first seven dates that will lead you down the aisle of holy matrimony. These seven "intellectual" dates will give you the design to keep your dating in the intellectual arena until the proper time for it to merge into the emotional arena. Your spirituality will give you a desire to keep your dating in the intellectual arena until the proper time for it to merge into the emotional arena. Develop your spirituality and let it govern your dating and all your life's decisions. A desire without a design is a recipe for failure. Allow your spiritual desire to employ this spiritual design and discover its merits.

Perhaps you will argue that no man will endure seven intellectual dates. The more you argue this, the more evidence you provide to prove how far we have fallen from progressive civility. Where are the Jacobs of our day who are willing to work seven years for a wife (see Genesis 29:18)? Men who are unwilling to make a "love deposit" for a good wife are not likely to be good husbands. Enduring (enjoying) seven dates is far easier than navigating the normal complexities of marriage.

Communication leads to friendship, which leads to compassion, which leads to commitment, which is essential for a healthy marriage.

I am not suggesting that these seven dates are the only way to matrimony. I do suggest, however, that from every angle it is obvious that communication leads to friendship, which leads to compassion, which leads to commitment, which is essential for a healthy marriage.

Here are the dos and do nots for these first seven dating experiences:

"Do nots" for the first seven dating experiences

- Do not bring him to your house.
- Do not go to his house.
- Do not meet at a restaurant.
- Do not go to a club.
- Do not go to any other social place where someone or something will provide entertainment. Avoid any third-party entertainers.

- Do not listen to music.

"Dos" for the first seven dating experiences

- Meet where you can look "eyeball to eyeball" and just talk.
- Meet at the park.
- Meet at the library.
- Meet at Barnes & Noble.
- Meet at Books-a-Million.
- Meet at any public place where you can talk with minimal distractions.

Take with you a $10 Starbucks gift card.

In the next section you will find specific information to help you prepare, go on, and process seven dates. There is information for "before the date"—questions to prepare; information for the date itself, and finally questions to help you evaluate each date. Between dates, engage in short communication only. Keep busy being single.

Remember, your goal is to keep dating in the intellectual realm, not the emotional realm, and this process will help you do it. Do remember that dating is to be a social experience not a scientific experience. Therefore variables change from time to time and from person to person.

While you are on your date, be prepared to answer the questions that you ask him. Occasionally you may share your answers to the questions even if he has not asked. The date provides your golden moment to shine forth your strengths.

If you have already been sexually active, during these seven dates do not talk about your sexual experiences. If the dating relationship proceeds healthily, there will be plenty of time to indulge in necessary conversation. Sex is a part of marriage. Sexual history may impact the marriage. If the dating proceeds toward marriage, you will need to have some conversations about sex.

If you have already enjoyed several pleasant dates with someone, I still recommend this "seven intellectual dates" concept so that you can establish your communication in the intellectual arena before you attempt to do so in the emotional arena. Even if you have been dating the same person for a while, I highly recommend this concept. If you have been dating for a while and wondering, "Where will this ultimately lead?" or "How can I get out of this rut of routine?" there is still hope for you. It is not too late for you to establish your communication in the intellectual arena before you wander further into the emotional arena.

If you have the resolve to speak the following face to face, then do so. If, however, you believe your words will be better received or understood in writing, then send this as a written note.

Dear _____,

I have been praying and thinking about our relationship. I have decided to change some things so that we can become better friends. This change will help our dating to become more spiritually progressive and in harmony with what God wants for us.

For the next several dates, we need to focus on intellectually getting to know each other and not invest our energy becoming emotionally charged. In order to do this, I will arrange our next several dates and they will not cost you any money at all.

I know this is different from what we have done, but trust me. I know that this is right for you and me. Therefore, this is what I must do. If you do not want to participate, I will understand. If that is the case, I wish you well and release you from all previous commitments.

Sincerely,

Chapter 6
FIRST DATE

Before the date

Visit the place where you will go on the date. If you are using a library conference room, make sure you can reserve it for the appropriate time. If you are going to the park, locate an appropriate place within view of other people. If you are going to another public place, make sure that you locate a place with minimal distractions.

First date should begin at least three hours before sunset. It should last no longer than two hours. Starting and ending the date early sends the message that you do have a life and something else to do. Early evening helps keep the date in the intellectual arena more so than the emotional arena. Also he will wonder if you might also have another pursuer. This just heightens his interest.

Prepare your questions

Prepare your questions before your date. Learn to ask opened ended questions and you can become the life of the party. Properly worded questions cause people to do what they do best: talk about themselves. Preparing a list of questions in advance will help you to do this. You may not ask all of them, but just ask enough of them to keep the conversations flowing. Find a way to compliment his responses to your questions. Your goal is not to ask questions as if it were an interview but as a casual conversation. A good way to ask a question is to say, "What do you think about _____?" Another good way to preface your question is to say, "Tell me about _____."

Faith questions

These may not seem like faith questions, but they are faith questions in that you are looking to discover to what faith system he subscribes. Does he believe in God? Does he honor what he believes about God?

- What are your favorite food and drink? How do you spend your time alone? Do you enjoy spending time alone?

- Tell me about your future aspirations. How satisfied are you with your career progression: income, benefits, job task, job location, work schedule, and personnel?

- What are your future educational goals?

- Who are your best male friends? What do you have in common? What core values do you share? What disagreements have you had recently with them?

- Who are your best female friends? What do you have in common? What core values do you share? What disagreements have you had recently with them?

Family questions

- Tell me about your father. What are some of your most cherished childhood memories and or experiences with your father? If your father was absent, what are some experiences that you would have loved to have enjoyed with your father?

- Tell me about the very first girl or girlfriend whom you remember liking. Why did you like her? How did you let her know that you liked her? How did she respond when she found out that you liked her?

Finance questions

- What is the last book you read about financial management?
- What is the most money you ever lost at one time? How did you lose it? How did you feel? What did you do to prevent losing money again?

Current event question

- You designate one to discuss:

_____

_____

Historical event question

- You designate one to discuss:

_____

_____

For the date

- He must provide his transportation.
- You provide your transportation.
- Meet him at the designated place.
- Arrive at least ten minutes early.

Dress and attire

Your spiritually compassionate and progressive thinking must overshadow him during the first date. In other words baffle him with your internal brilliance not your external beauty. Therefore dress casually comfortable. Do not wear revealing or provocative clothing. Do not even wear figure-flattering clothing. If you make an intellectual connection, you will enjoy numerous occasions wearing figure-flattering and provocative clothing—after the wedding. Do have your natural hair styled. You may style your natural hair as professionally progressive as you desire.

During the date

On the first date, greet him with a warm and inviting smile. Do not greet him with a physical embrace. Give a one-shake handshake only if he extends his hand. I know this is severely outdated for most and somewhat stilted for the rest but once again this is just a common-sense intentional approach to connect intellectually before becoming emotionally intertwined. This does not suggest that a hug always starts hormones racing out of control, but rather just a word of caution.

Sit opposite him. Attentively observe his physical expressions and body movements. Notice his tone and emphasis of voice. Just talk and listen to him talk for the duration of two hours. Do not bombard him with questions. Skillfully weave questions into the conversation. Do not disagree with any statements he makes. However you may ask questions for clarification and/or to deepen the conversation. Encourage him to talk about himself, his family, and his aspirations. Do remember exactly what he says and how he says what he says. There are not necessarily right and wrong answers. His answers either give you insight into his heart or they fail to give you insight into his heart. His answers give you an opportunity to determine the extent of your present compatibility.

If the date did not progress well enough to date again, thank him for coming. Tell him that you appreciate him sharing his time and of himself, give him the $10.00 Starbucks gift card (or some other small token of appreciation) and say goodbye. Men love receiving gifts. Far too often, men are viewed as the giver not the recipient. The gift will indicate that you are a compassionate woman and enable him more easily accept your no to future dates.

If on the other hand he proved to be a spiritually compassionate and progressive thinker, and the date progressed well enough to date again, invite him to Starbucks for coffee and a cinnamon roll. Remind him that the expense of the date is on you. He must drive his own vehicle to Starbucks. Ask him what he would like. Order and pay for the food and bring it to the table. If he insists on paying, do not make a scene. Allow him to do so.

Do not remain at Starbucks more than thirty minutes; 150 minutes is enough time to spend on the first date. Say to him, "I have enjoyed the evening. If you desire, we can do this again three weeks from now." Do not offer any reason for the three-week delay. If he insists, the only reason that you should give him is that you will not be available until then. Please do not kiss him nor hug him on the first date. You may give him a one-hand handshake. Immediately get into your car and drive away without comment.

Evaluation

After you return home from the date, write what you discovered. Be as specific as you can remember. Note the plusses and minuses of each response. Do not be overly technical, however. Remember this is a social date not a scientific experiment. You are in the library not the laboratory. Your goal is to gather information about him as well as share information about yourself. You are searching for what common interests, level of compatibility, and future similar intentions you may have.

Faith question

_____

_____

_____

Family question

_____

_____

_____

Finance question

_____

_____

_____

Current event question

_____

_____

_____

Other pertinent or memorable information

_____

_____

_____

Chapter 7

SECOND DATE

Arrange the date

Call him and ask if he would like to go on another date. Do not email or text to arrange the second date, although you may do for future dates. Invite him to accompany you to volunteer your services to help seniors. You may volunteer your services at a nursing home, assisted-living facility, or a retirement home. Or you can choose one senior citizen and assist in their home. If you visit in the home, you may wash dishes, clean house, cut grass, or perform any other chores. Or you can invite him to participate in any service-oriented activity. Doing something (ministry) for someone else is an excellent way to discover the altruistic spirit within a man. Men tend to talk more while they are engaged in an activity than when they are sitting idle. Not only will this serve a window to help you look into his soul, but it will also stimulate deeper conversation.

Before the date

Obtain permission and arrange for all the necessary items.

Prepare your questions

Faith questions

- What is your greatest asset? What is your greatest relationship asset? What is your greatest accomplishment?

How has it enhanced your self-esteem and/or self-concept the most? Of which accomplishment are you most proud? Why? What lasting impact has and will that accomplishment have upon you? To what extent do you attribute your success to the help of God?

- Tell me about your success/accomplishment of which you are most proud. You may nurture him to explore by asking the following: How did those who were supportive respond to you? How did those who were unsupportive respond to you? How did you respond to those who were unsupportive? Why do you think they were unsupportive? What lasting impact did you receive from the whole experience?

Family questions

- Tell me about your mother. What are some of your most cherished childhood memories and or experiences with your mother? If your mother was absent, what are some experiences that you would have loved to have enjoyed with your mother?

Finance question

- What is the most money you ever earned and/or accumulated in a short period of time? How did you receive it? How did you feel?

Current event question

- You designate one to discuss:

_____

_____

Historical event question

- You designate one to discuss:

_____

_____

For the date

- He must provide his transportation.
- You provide your transportation.
- Meet him at the designated place.
- Arrive at least ten minutes early.

Dress and attire

Your spiritually compassionate and progressive thinking must over-shadow him during the second date as well. In other words continue to baffle him with your internal brilliance not your external beauty. Dress casually comfortable. Do not wear revealing nor provocative clothing. Do not even wear figure-flattering clothing. If you make an intellectual connection, you will enjoy numerous occasions wearing figure-flattering and provocative clothing—after the wedding. Do have your natural hair styled. You may style your natural hair as professionally progressive as you desire.

During the date

On the second date, greet him with a warm and inviting smile. You may offer a two-shake handshake. Do not offer to greet him with a physical embrace. If he offers a hug, give him a side-to-side shoulder hug only.

Notice how joyfully he serves during the nursing home visit. While you are working weave pertinent questions into your conversation. Do not disagree with any statement that he makes. However you may ask questions for clarification and/or to deepen the conversation. Encourage him to talk about himself, his family, and his aspirations. Do remember exactly what he says and how he says what he says. Do not bombard with questions. Skillfully weave questions into the conversation. Proceed not as if it is an interview but as a casual conversation.

If the date did not progress well enough to date again, thank him for coming. Tell him that you appreciate him sharing his time and of himself, give him his $10.00 Starbucks gift card and say goodbye.

If he has continued to be a spiritually compassionate and progressive thinker and the date did progress well enough to date again, invite him to Starbucks for coffee and a cinnamon roll. Remind him that the expense of the date is on you. He must drive his own vehicle to Starbucks. Ask him what he would like. Order and pay for the food and bring it to the table.

Do not remain at Starbucks more than forty-five minutes. Say to him, "I have enjoyed the evening. If you desire, we can do this again two weeks from now." Do not offer any reason for the two-week delay. If he insists, the only reason that you should give him is that you will not be available until then. Please do not kiss him nor hug him on the second date. You may give him a two-shake handshake. Immediately get into your car and drive away without comment.

Evaluation

After you return home from the date, write what you discovered. Be as specific as you can remember. Note the plusses and minuses of each response. Do not be overly technical, however. Remember this is a social date not a scientific experiment. You are in the library not the laboratory. Your goal is to gather information about him as well as share information about yourself. You are searching for what common interests, level of compatibility, and future similar intentions you may have.

Faith question

_____

_____

_____

Family question

_____

_____

_____

Finance question

_____

_____

_____

Current event question

_____

_____

_____

Other pertinent or memorable information

_____

_____

_____

Chapter 8

THIRD DATE

Arrange the date

Call him and ask if he would like to go out on another date. Remind him that he will incur no financial cost. You will cover the full cost of the date. If he accepts, invite him to the place of your choosing. Choose a different setting from the first date.

Before the date

Visit the place where you will go on the date. If you are using a library conference room, make sure that you can reserve if for the appropriate time. If you are going to the park, locate an appropriate place within view of other people. If you are going to another public place, make sure that you locate a place with minimal distractions.

The third date should begin at least one hour before sunset. It should last no longer than two hours. Starting and ending the date early sends the message that you do have a life and something else to do. Early evening helps keep the date in the intellectual arena rather than the emotional arena. Also he will wonder if you might also have another pursuer.

Prepare your questions

Faith questions

- What has been your greatest setback? Which of your failures/disappointments have impacted your self-esteem and/or self-concept the most? Why? What lasting impact has and will that experience have upon you? What strategies did you use and will you use to minimize the harmful impact? To what extent do you attribute that experience to the devil, satanic influence, and/or the absence of the favor of God?

- You may elicit information by saying, "Tell me about the failure/disappointment of which you are most unhappy." You may nurture him to explore his own heart and feelings toward adversaries by asking the following: How did those who were supportive of you respond to you? How did those who were happy about your failure respond to you? How did you respond to those who were happy about your failure? Why do you think they were glad that you failed? What lasting impact did you receive from the whole experience?

Family questions

- Tell me about your brothers and sisters. What are some of your most cherished childhood memories and or experiences with them? If they were absent, what are some experiences that you would have loved to have enjoyed with them? From your relationship with them, what aspirations do you have for your children?

- When was the longest time you practiced celibacy? Why?

Finance question

- What do you think about taxation in America? Who should pay taxes? How much should people pay? What are your views about the flat tax? What are your views about tax deductions within the IRS code? What are your views about the way tax revenue is spent by our government?

Current event question

- You designate one to discuss:

_____

_____

Historical event question

- You designate one to discuss:

_____

_____

For the date

- He must provide his transportation.
- You provide your transportation.
- Meet him at the designated place.
- Arrive at least ten minutes early.

Dress and attire

Your spiritually compassionate and progressive thinking must overshadow him during the third date as well. In other words continue to baffle him with your internal brilliance not your external beauty. Dress casually comfortable. Do not wear revealing nor provocative clothing. Do not even wear figure-flattering clothing. If you make an intellectual connection, you will enjoy numerous occasions wearing figure-flattering and provocative clothing—after the wedding. Do have your natural hair styled. You may style your natural hair as professionally progressive as you desire.

During the date

On the third date, greet him with a warm and inviting smile. You may offer a shoulder-to-shoulder hug. Do not offer to greet him with a face-to-face breast-to-chest embrace. If he offers that type of hug, avoid it.

Sit opposite him. Attentively observe his physical expressions and body movements. Notice his tone and emphasis of voice. Just talk and listen to him talk for the duration of two hours. Do not disagree with any statement that he makes. However you may ask questions for clarification and/or to deepen the conversation. Encourage him to talk about himself, his family, and his aspirations. Do remember exactly what he says and how he says what he says. Do not bombard him with questions. Skillfully weave questions into the conversation. Proceed not as if it were an interview but as a casual conversation.

If the date did not progress well enough to date again, thank him for coming. Tell him that you appreciate him sharing his time and of himself, give him his $10.00 Starbucks gift card and say goodbye.

If he has continued to be a spiritually compassionate and progressive thinker and the date did progress well enough to date again, invite him to Starbucks for coffee and a cinnamon roll. Remind him that the expense of the date is on you. He must drive his own vehicle to Starbucks. Ask him what he would like. Order and pay for the food and bring it to the table.

Do not remain at Starbucks more than sixty minutes. Say to him, "I have enjoyed the evening; if you desire, we can do this again one week from now." Do not offer any reason for the one-week delay. If he insists, the only reason that you should give him is that you will not be available until then. Please do not kiss him nor hug him on the third date. You may give him a two-shake handshake. Immediately get into your car and drive away without comment.

Evaluation

After you return home from the date, write what you discovered. Be as specific as you can remember. Note the plusses and minuses of each response. Do not be overly technical, however. Remember this is a social date not a scientific experiment. You are in the library not the laboratory. Your goal is to gather information about him as well as share information about yourself. You are searching for what common interests, level of compatibility, and future similar intentions you may have.

Faith question

_____

_____

_____

Family question

_____

_____

_____

Finance question

_____

_____

_____

Current event question

_____

_____

_____

Other pertinent or memorable information

_____

_____

_____

Chapter 9

FOURTH DATE

Arrange the date

Call him and ask if he would like to go on another date. Invite him to accompany you to volunteer your services to help children. You may volunteer your services at a children's hospital, public school classroom, chaperone a children school trip, assist mentally or physically challenged children, etc. You may take gifts and serve.

Before the date

Obtain permission and arrange for all the necessary items.

Prepare your questions

Faith questions

- What are your thoughts about God? Does God exist? What is God like? If you believe that God does not exist, would you like for a God to exist? How did the world come to believe that God exists? Describe the kind of God that you would like to exist?

Family questions

- Tell me about a time when you were most angry? How did you overcome your anger? When were you most angry with a female? Why? How did you overcome it? (For your insights, read my book *Good and Angry*, a personal guide to anger management that provides a spiritual perspective of anger.)

- What is the greatest positive that you bring to a relationship? What is the meanest thing you have ever said and/ or done to a woman? How did you express repentance? What is the kindest thing you ever did for a woman?

- Tell me about the hurts that you remember most from your childhood. You may nurture him to explore unresolved issues from childhood by asking the following: Why have you remembered this so vividly? How do you feel when you now think about it?

Finance questions

- If the smoke alarm sounded and your house was on fire, what seven things would you attempt to take with you as you exited? Why?

Current event question

- You designate one to discuss:

_____

_____

Historical event question

- You designate one to discuss:

_____

_____

For the date

- He must provide his transportation.
- You provide your transportation.
- Meet him at the designated place.

Dress and attire

Your spiritually compassionate and progressive thinking must over-shadow him during the fourth date as well. In other words continue to baffle him with your internal brilliance not your external beauty. Dress casually comfortable. Do not wear revealing nor provoca-tive clothing. Do not even wear figure-flattering clothing. If you make an intellectual connection, you will enjoy numerous occa-sions wearing figure-flattering and provocative clothing—after the wedding. Do have your natural hair styled. You may style your natural hair as professionally progressive as you desire.

During the date

On the fourth date, greet him with a warm and inviting smile. You may offer a shoulder-to-shoulder hug. Do not offer to greet him with a face-to-face breast-to-chest embrace. If he offers that type of hug, avoid it.

Notice how joyfully he serves. While you are working, weave pertinent questions into your conversation. Do not disagree with any statement he makes. However you may ask questions for clarification and/or to deepen the conversation. Encourage him to talk about himself, his family, and his aspirations. Do remember exactly what he says and how he says what he says. Do not bombard him with questions. Skillfully weave questions into the conversation. Proceed not as if it is an interview but as a casual conversation.

If the date did not progress well enough to date again, thank him for coming. Tell him that you appreciate him sharing his time and of himself, give him his $10.00 Starbucks gift card and say goodbye.

If he has continued to be a spiritually compassionate and progressive thinker and the date did progress well enough to date again, invite him to Starbucks for coffee and a cinnamon roll. Remind him that the expense of the date is on you. He must drive his own vehicle to Starbucks. Ask him what he would like. Order and pay for the food and bring it to the table.

Do not remain at Starbucks more than sixty minutes. Say to him, "I have enjoyed the evening, if you desire, we can do this again one week from now." Do not offer any reason for the one-week delay.

If he insists, the only reason that you should give him is that you will not be available until then. Please do not kiss him nor hug him on the fourth date. You may give him a two-shake handshake. Immediately get into your car and drive away without comment.

Evaluation

After you return home from the date, write what you discovered. Be as specific as you can remember. Note the plusses and minuses of each response. Do not be overly technical, however. Remember this is a social date not a scientific experiment. You are in the library not the laboratory. Your goal is to gather information about him as well as share information about yourself. You are searching for what common interests, level of compatibility, and future similar intentions you may have.

Faith question

_____

_____

_____

Family question

_____

_____

_____

Finance question

_____

_____

_____

Current event question

_____

_____

_____

Other pertinent or memorable information

_____

_____

_____

Chapter 10

FIFTH DATE

Arrange the date

Call him and ask if he would like to go out on another date. Remind him that he will incur no financial cost. You will cover the full cost of the date. If he accepts, invite him to the place of your choosing.

Before the date

Visit the place where you will go on the date. If you are using a library conference room, make sure that you can reserve if for the appropriate time. If you are going to the park, locate an appropriate place within view of other people. If you are going to another public place, make sure that you locate a place with minimal distractions.

The fifth date should begin at least by sunset. It should last no longer than three hours.

Prepare your questions

Faith questions

- What are your thoughts about Jesus Christ? Which of His teachings do you admire? Which teachings have questions about? What behavior of Jesus captures your attention? What do you think about His death and resurrection? If you do not believe in Jesus, would the world be better off if there had been a Jesus?

Family questions

- Do you think you will ever get married? Why would you want to get married? If you met a woman who met all your preferred criteria in a wife, would you marry her within twelve months? If not, by what date? What would be the hindrance?

Finance question

- What do you think about insurance and investments? How well are you preparing?

Current event question

- You designate one to discuss:

_____

_____

Historical event question

- You designate one to discuss:

_____

_____

For the date

- He must provide his transportation.
- You provide your transportation.

- Meet him at the designated place.
- Arrive at least ten minutes early.

Dress and attire

Your spiritually compassionate and progressive thinking must overshadow him during the fifth date as well. In other words continue to baffle him with your internal brilliance not your external beauty. Dress casually comfortable. Do not wear revealing nor provocative clothing. Do not even wear figure-flattering clothing. If you make an intellectual connection, you will enjoy numerous occasions wearing figure-flattering and provocative clothing—after the wedding. Do have your natural hair styled. You may style your natural hair as professionally progressive as you desire.

During the date

On the fifth date, greet him with a warm and inviting smile. You may offer a face-to-face hug. Sit opposite him. Attentively observe his physical expressions and body movements. Notice his tone and emphasis of voice. Just talk and listen to him talk for the duration of three hours. Do not disagree with any statement that he makes. However you may ask questions for clarification and/or to deepen the conversation. Encourage him to talk about himself, his family, and his aspirations. Do remember exactly what he says and how he says what he says it. Do not bombard him with questions. Skillfully weave questions into the conversation. Proceed not as if it is an interview but as a casual conversation.

If the date did not progress well enough to date again, thank him for coming. Tell him that you appreciate him sharing his time and of himself, give him his $10.00 Starbucks gift card and say goodbye.

If he has continued to be a spiritually compassionate and progressive thinker and the date did progress well enough to date again, allow him to choose dinner so that you may continue to talk. Do not attend a movie, a club, or any place that will interfere with talking.

Afterwards, say to him, "I have enjoyed the evening. If you desire, we can do this again whenever you choose." Please do not kiss him nor hug him on the fifth date. You may give him a two-shake handshake. Immediately get into your car and drive away without comment.

Evaluation

After you return home from the date, write what you discovered. Be as specific as you can remember. Note the plusses and minuses of each response. Do not be overly technical, however. Remember this is a social date not a scientific experiment. You are in the library not the laboratory. Your goal is to gather information about him as well as share information about yourself. You are searching for what common interests, level of compatibility, and future similar intentions you may have.

Faith question

_____

_____

_____

Family question

_____

_____

_____

Finance question

_____

_____

_____

Current event question

_____

_____

_____

Other pertinent or memorable information

_____

_____

_____

Since you are dating to become married, his answers to these questions are of paramount importance: "Do you think you will ever get married? Why would you want to get married? If you met a woman who met all your preferred criteria in a wife, would you marry her within twelve months? If not, by what date? What would be the hindrance?"

What was his exact response?

_____

_____

_____

_____

_____

Anything other than twelve months or a definite time fails to warrant another date. He is either non-committal or not on the track with you at this time.

Chapter 11

SIXTH DATE

Arrange the date

Call him and ask if he would like to go out on another date. Inform him that you will accompany him to the service opportunity of his choosing. He must arrange for all the service items and other details.

Before the date

Read the word of God, pray, and meditate upon spiritual truths. Reflect upon the previous dates and the intellectual bonding that this process has produced. Consider whom you will share this with.

Think about what you should have said differently. What should you have said that went unsaid? What answers or comments from him are yet unclear? Write a thank you letter to one married female who has positively impacted your life.

Prepare your questions

Faith questions

- What are your thoughts about church? What do you like most? What do you like least?

Family question

- What is your dream sheet for your children?

Finance question

- What are your thoughts about retirements and wills?

Current event question

- You designate one to discuss:

Historical event question

- You designate one to discuss:

For the date

You can ride together.

Dress and attire

Your spiritually compassionate and progressive thinking must overshadow him during the sixth date as well. In other words continue to baffle him with your internal brilliance not your external beauty. Dress casually comfortable. Do not wear revealing nor provocative clothing. Do not even wear figure-flattering clothing. If you make an intellectual connection, you will enjoy numerous occasions wearing figure-flattering and provocative clothing—after the wedding. Do have your natural hair styled. You may style your natural hair as professionally progressive as you desire.

During the date

On the sixth date, greet him with a warm and inviting smile. You may offer a face-to-face hug. Notice how joyfully he serves. While you are working weave pertinent questions into your conversation. Do not disagree with any statement that he makes. However you may ask questions for clarification and/or to deepen the conversation. Encourage him to talk about himself, his family, and his aspirations. Do remember exactly what he says and how he says what he says it. Do not bombard him with questions. Skillfully weave questions into the conversation. Proceed not as if it is an interview but as a casual conversation.

If the date did not progress well enough to date again, thank him for coming. Tell him that you appreciate him sharing his time and of himself, give him his $10.00 Starbucks gift card and say goodbye.

If he has continued to be a spiritually compassionate and progressive thinker and the date did progress well enough to date again, allow him to choose dinner so that you may continue to talk. Do not attend a movie, a club, or any place that will interfere with talking

Afterward say to him, "I have enjoyed the evening. If you desire, we can do this again whenever you choose." Let him pick the time and place but tell him you prefer a place where you can talk rather than a movie, club, sporting event, or any place that interferes with talking. Please do not kiss him nor hug him on the sixth date. You may give him a two-shake handshake. Immediately get into your car and drive away without comment.

Evaluation

After you return home from the date, write what you discovered. Be as specific as you can remember. Note the plusses and minuses of each response. Do not be overly technical, however. Remember this is a social date not a scientific experiment. You are in the library not the laboratory. Your goal is to gather information about him as well as share information about yourself. You are searching for what common interests, level of compatibility, and future similar intentions you may have.

Faith question

_____

_____

_____

Family question

_____

_____

_____

Finance question

_____

_____

_____

Current event question

_____

_____

_____

Other pertinent or memorable information

_____

_____

_____

Chapter 12

SEVENTH DATE

Arrange the date

- He arranges the date.
- Date may start at any time but end by 10:30 p.m.
- He must provide transportation.
- He must pick you up at your residence.

Before the date

Read the word of God, pray and meditate upon spiritual truths. Reflect upon the previous dates and what the future dates may be like. Do consider where this may ultimately lead.

Think about what you should have said differently. What should you have said that went unsaid? What answers or comments from him are yet unclear? Write a thank you letter to one married male who has positively impacted your life.

Prepare your questions

Faith question

- What are your thoughts about spirituality? What do you believe about God as the creator? What do you think about the Bible? How valid is its teachings? How relevant is it for your life?

Family question

- What age should boys begin to date? What age should girls begin to date? What are your thoughts about coed college dorms?

Finance question

- What are your thoughts about prenuptial agreements?

Current event question

- You designate one to discuss:

  _____

  _____

Historical event question

- You designate one to discuss:

  _____

  _____

For the date

Intentionally be twenty minutes late. You are testing his patience. Near the end of the date, explain why you were late so that he will know that tardiness is not one of your character flaws.

He must open and close your doors. Wait inside the car until he comes around and opens the door.

Dress and attire

Your spiritually compassionate and progressive thinking must over-shadow him during this and all future dates as well. In other words continue to baffle him with your internal brilliance not your external beauty. Dress casually comfortable. Do not wear revealing nor provocative clothing. Do not even wear figure-flattering clothing. If you make an intellectual connection, you will enjoy numerous occasions wearing figure-flattering and provocative clothing—after the wedding. Do have your natural hair styled. You may style your natural hair as professionally progressive as you desire.

During the date

On the seventh date, greet him with a warm and inviting smile. You may offer a face-to-face hug. You may sit beside him. Attentively observe his physical expressions and body movements. Notice his tone and emphasis of voice. Just talk and listen to him talk for the duration of the date. Do not disagree with any statement that he makes. However you may ask questions for clarification and/or to deepen the conversation. Encourage him to talk about himself, his family, and his aspirations. Do remember exactly what he says and how he says what he says. Do not bombard him with questions. Skillfully weave questions into the conversation. Proceed not as if it is an interview but as a casual conversation.

If the date did not progress well enough to date again, thank him for coming. Tell him that you appreciate him sharing his time and of himself, give him his $10.00 Starbucks gift card and say goodbye.

If he has continued to be a spiritually compassionate and progressive thinker and the date did progress well enough to date again, allow him to choose dinner so that you may continue to talk. Do not attend a movie, club, or any other place that will interfere with talking.

Let him ask for the next date—but do oblige.

Evaluation

After you return home from the date, write what you discovered. Be as specific as you can remember. Note the plusses and minuses of each response. Do not be overly technical, however. Remember this is a social date not a scientific experiment. You are in the library not the laboratory. Your goal is to gather information about him as well as share information about yourself. You are searching for what common interests, level of compatibility, and future similar intentions you may have.

Faith question

_____

_____

_____

Family question

_____

_____

_____

Finance question

_____

_____

_____

Current event question

_____

_____

_____

Other pertinent or memorable information

_____

_____

_____

In the process of these seven dates, you will have gathered much information about him as well as shared much information about yourself. How do you process it? Remember that this book is a social experience not a scientific one. Therefore there is not a definite paradigm in which to place this information. For that reason I will not tell you what to look for nor how to process the information discovered. However look for trends. For example, how does he process anger? Does anger linger for unusually long periods of time? Are there violent explosions throughout his life?

Just being able to talk for long periods of time is a plus. Definitely being able to open up and talk about heart-felt issues in a nonthreatening way will help you evaluate the time you have spent together and the conversations you have shared. Listen to what has been said and what may intentionally not have been said.

In addition to trends and long conversations, identify his behaviors that will irritate you. Do you see indicators of improvement? Also, identify behaviors that will bring pleasure to you. Do you see indicators of them remaining and increasing?

You are seeking to know if this man has the capacity to love you and be your head as God has so decreed (see Ephesians chapter 5). You are searching to know if you can willingly submit to this man as God has so decreed (1 Peter chapter 3).

If you discover that your date is more spiritual in his thinking than you are, just praise the Lord. But do seek God's wisdom so that you will know if this is God's choice for you. Pray and ask others to pray for your insight. If you have kept intellectual control of your emotions, you will very likely see much more clearly. Your utmost scrutiny is required if you choose to proceed further. Remember, the choice you make now will determine whether you have a lifetime of marital misery or bliss.

Chapter 13

QUEENS WHO FOUND THEIR KINGS

I F YOU HAVE read through this book, I have succeeded. Even if you discard everything I have said, I have still had a margin of success. The special effort that you will have to exert to discard what I have said indicates some success. Confucius, the wise Chinese thinker and social philosopher who was born in 551 BC, said, "No real learning takes place until two conflicting minds rub together."

Herbert and Zelmyra Fisher

If my words have not convinced you, at least allow the practical wisdom of the world's longest living married couple to have a place in your heart. Herbert and Zelmyra Fisher of North Carolina were married for eighty-six years and held the Guinness World Record for the longest marriage of any living couple. Herbert recently passed away at age 105; Zelmyra is 103 years old. On Valentine's Day a few years ago, they teamed up with Twitter to answer relationship questions.[6]

Please read their words and take them to heart:

> Q: What made you realize that you could spend the rest of your lives together? Were you scared at all?
>
> A: With each day that passed, our relationship was more solid and secure. Divorce was never an option—or even a thought.

Q: How did you know your spouse was the right one for you?

A: We grew up together and were best friends before we married. A friend is for life—our marriage has lasted a lifetime.

Q: Is there anything you would do differently after more than eighty years of marriage?

A: We wouldn't change a thing. There's no secret to our marriage. We just did what was needed for each other and our family.

Q: What is your advice to someone who is trying to keep the faith that Mr. Right is really out there?

A: (Zelmyra) Mine was just around the corner! He is never too far away, so keep the faith. When you meet him, you'll know.

Q: What was the best piece of marriage advice you ever received?

A: Respect, support, and communicate with each other. Be faithful, honest, and true. Love each other with all your heart.

Q: What are the most important attributes of a good spouse?

A: (Zelmyra) A hard worker and good provider. The 1920s were hard, but Herbert wanted and provided the best for us. I married a good man!

Q: What is your best Valentine's Day memory?

A: (Zelmyra) I cook dinner every day. Herbert left work early and surprised me—he cooked dinner for me! He is a *very* good cook!

(Herbert) I said that I was going to cook dinner for her and she could relax—the look on her face and clean plate made my day!

Q: You got married very young—how did you both manage to grow as individuals yet not grow apart as a couple?

A: "Everyone who plants a seed and harvests the crop celebrates together." We are individuals, but accomplish more together.

Q: What is your fondest memory of your eighty-five-year marriage?

A: Our legacy: Five children, ten grandchildren, nine great-grandchildren, and one great-great grandchild.

Q: Does communicating get easier with time? How do you keep your patience?

A: The children are grown, so we talk more now. We can enjoy our time on the porch or our rocking chairs—together.

Q: How did you cope when you had to be physically separated for long periods of time?

A: (Herbert) We were apart for two months when Zelmyra was hospitalized with our fifth child. It was the most difficult time of my life. Zelmyra's mother helped me with the house and the other children; otherwise I would have lost my mind.

Q: At the end of a bad relationship day, what is the most important thing to remind yourselves?

A: Remember marriage is not a contest—never keep a score. God has put the two of you together on the same team to win.

Q: Is fighting important?

A: Never physically! Agree that it's okay to disagree and fight for what really matters. Learn to bend—not break!

Q: What's the one thing you have in common that transcends everything else?

A: We are both Christians and believe in God. Marriage is a commitment to the Lord. We pray with and for each other every day.

David and Sandra

Before I knew them, David and Sandra decided to date the spiritual way. Before going on a date, they would pray together that God would govern their thoughts and actions. For insurance, they only dated with other couples never alone.

Several years ago, after twenty years of marriage, David spoke at a family conference on the subject, "I waited and I am glad I did." His personal testimony in his presentation continues to bless the lives of those who heard it. Now after more than thirty years of marriage, they enjoy a most admirable marriage. Their compassionate care for each other is just breathtaking.

Milton and Rachel

Milton and Rachel are a novel couple. They met at a church event and for more than a year they dated the spiritual way. Honoring God was immensely important to them both throughout their courtship. They avoided physical intimacy, instead engaging in activities that were both fun and spiritually edifying. They spent time with other Christian friends, went to movies, restaurants, and always prayed and studied together. In fact Rachel often states the moment she fell in love with Milton was when she heard him praying to God that he would always seek her highest spiritual well-being. Now after ten years of marriage, Rachel regularly expands her vocabulary so that she can describe the joy brought to her by her husband.

Here is what Rachel posted on a social media network as she and Milton celebrated their tenth year of marriage: "Today, I'm thankful to God to be able to celebrate ten years of marriage to the most loving, noble, kind, and Spirit-filled man I know. He's an incredible provider, protector, patient, and is the type of man who would give his life for me without thinking. God has truly blessed us with ten years of His love and goodness, and I am most thankful."

Shannon and Twanda

Twanda met Shannon on a blind date at church through a mutual friend. After a few months they realized they were compatible for each other and wanted to continue the relationship. "We dated for over a year," Twanda says, "with dating boundaries such as no sexual intimacy and no company past 10:00 p.m. This really helped us to do what God intended and we became more spiritually connected than emotionally connected. After eleven years of marriage, we became each other's best friend. He knows my innermost secrets. We have a mutual respect for each other and an understanding to know what each other is lacking in the relationship. This helps us to support our weaknesses and encourage our strengths. The most valuable gift my husband gives me is his time. I continually thank God for a loving and spiritual husband."

David and Jean

David and Jean knew each other in high school. They lost contact with each other after graduation but Jean's best friend would see

David occasionally, and Jean would ask her friend to say "hello" for her. "In 1997 we reconnected," Jean explains. "We started talking and spending time together—not much time because of our work schedules. In the time we spent together, I realized he was a man of integrity, a hard worker, a man of God, active in church and loved his mother. Before we made a true commitment to each other and marriage, we discussed and agreed on God's plan for our life: marriage, family, and children. We both believe our marriage was made by God. Communication, trust, and faith are what gets us through day to day, good and bad, sad and happy times."

Benny and Chiquita

In 1993 Benny and I met on the University of Mississippi campus where we were both working. He met me in the spring while I was running an errand in his office building. Later he called to ask me to lunch. I said yes and he hung up. It would be three months before we saw each other again. I said, "Mr. Walls don't you owe me lunch?" We had our first official date during the Christmas holidays of that same year.

We dated for two years and we had fun! We talked every day. We traveled on the weekends. We argued, laughed, cried, shared our dreams and secrets, learned new things, stressed over our lack of money, celebrated everything with ice cream from Baskin-Robbins, and even got our first dog. The main thing is that we bonded. We became best friends.

Because we were best friends, and we knew it, we declared ourselves in love and eloped with the help of Harold Redd and Jerry Taylor. We went to Memphis on a Saturday morning and "got hitched" in the backseat of Harold Redd's navy-blue Cadillac at the K-Mart parking lot on Highway 55 in Southaven, Mississippi. Jerry was the best man and he sat in the front seat with Harold. Benny and I were in the back seat. Although we never got rings, we made a commitment to God and to each other to make it work. We were married on August 10, 1996.

With marriage for Benny came two teenage stepdaughters, Candayce and Constance, more traveling and preaching workshops, recording jobs and his introduction to the shape note singing tradition. We had our everyday life struggles but we were in love.

In 2001 Benny completed his Master of Science degree in organizational development from American University in Washington, DC. He worked for several months as the interim campus minister at the student center with the Oxford Church of Christ. In 2004, he accepted a position as minister of involvement with the Ross Road Church of Christ in Memphis and we moved to Olive Branch, Mississippi. We returned to Oxford in 2007. Despite failing health, he continued speaking, writing, recording, and sharing the gospel at every opportunity. Our last project together was creating the Encouragement to Live internet radio station on www.Live365.com and the Encouragement to Live web page.

Benny and I experienced many trials and tribulations but God brought us through every one, a little stronger for the wear and tear. We were a match made in Heaven.

A friend summed it up best: "You two were always reinventing yourselves." It was true. We were always reinventing ourselves. We took projects as a team—whether it was driving on a road trip, remodeling the house, cooking a meal, preparing a lesson, recording an event or duplicating CDs. He was the master and I was his apprentice.

Ours is a love story that is a gift from God. We put God as the head of our relationship. We prayed over every decision that we would do what God would have us to do. Our mission in life was to be faithful to God and each other. And God blessed us beyond measure. Benny's was a life well lived and I am grateful to be part of it, even if it was only for a brief seventeen years. Blessed be the name of the Lord for His grace to both of us.

Dear Benny,

The past few days have been the hardest days of my life. I am honest when I say I never saw it coming. I believed until the end that you were going to come home and that we would bet back in our usual routine. Your passing has left me confused, hurt, and just outright grief-stricken to say the least. The fact that I am now a widow is unreal to me. Family and friends tell me that I will get through this and I know I will but it is still a "hard row to hoe."

You always taught me that when the going gets rough that we should count our blessings. This morning as I sit here writing this, I am taking some time to share with others how you blessed my life in so many ways.

First, you blessed my life by introducing me to the gospel of Jesus Christ. I grew up in a Christian Methodist Episcopal church with lots of time spent in the Baptist church. My mother bought me a set of children's Bible stories when I was young, so I had a good foundation of who was in the Bible and their exploits. But it was you who helped me to understand the gospel message and now the whole Bible was connected with one central theme that God so loved the world that He sent His son to die on the cross for the sins of man. Because of your patient teaching and explanations on grace, truth, obedience, and servanthood, I became a baptized believer. My entry into Heaven will be because God used you to bring me to Him That is my greatest blessing and I have you to thank for it. Thank you.

Second, you blessed my life by believing in me. I had such a low self-esteem; sometimes I could not even look people in the eye. I was self-conscious about myself and quite shy and bashful around people. You helped me to overcome so much. You helped me to understand and believe that I was a new creature in Christ and that I am loved by God and you. I was thinking about all the times I would get stressed over some task or program I was facing. You would always remind me, "Chiquita, you can do this." My mantra became, "I can do all things in Christ who strengthens me." I will take that with me forever no matter where I go.

Finally, you blessed me by setting an example to love people. I never knew anyone who loved people and reached out to people the way you did. You introduced me to a whole new world of family: biological family, church family, Southwestern Christian College family, and much more. Your friends became my friends. I became more than just Benny's wife. I developed into a recognized and beloved member of the Benny Walls' family circle. I grew to love being in this great clan of family that you had created that included all races, ages, and genders, religious and economic backgrounds. Because of you, I have sisters and brothers who love me from the east coast to the west coast and all over. Because of you, I learned to reach out to others in acts of kindness and support. I learned to love unconditionally and to make relations a priority at every turn.

The list could go on forever but I close now. I just want to say thank you for being my best friend ever. I pray that God will allow me to continue in your tradition to reach out and show love to the world around me.

Your girl, Chiquita

Benny Walls went home to be with the Lord on August 31, 2011.

Embrace the wisdom of those who have successfully married. Sense the joy they now experience. Why would you not trade your temporary pleasures and present frustration for the permanent pleasure that Zelmyra, Sandra, Twanda, Rachel, Jean, and Chiquita have enjoyed for so many years? Decide to replace that which is good for that which is better.

May you take the words of this book into your heart and may God bless your marriage.

ENDNOTES

1 Not their real names

2 Not his real name

3 Not her real name

4 *I Kissed Dating Goodbye,* by Joshua Harris (Multnomah, 1997)

5 Not her real name

6 www.twitter.com/longestmarried

PREVIOUS BOOKS
BY JOHN MARSHALL

Good and Angry

The Power of the Tongue

God, Listen!

Final Answer

Success Is a God Idea

Show Me the Money

God Knows

My God

Faith, Family, and Finances (Volume 1)

Faith, Family, and Finances (Volume 2)

Walking with God (Bible school curriculum)

JOHN MARSHALL

JOHN DAVIS MARSHALL, the grandson of a former slave, was born and raised in Medon (just outside of Jackson), Tennessee. He mentors men, serves as a relationship consultant, a facilitator for conflict resolution, and is pastor of Graceview Church in Stone Mountain, Georgia.

A visionary leader, he has served as minister for churches in Alabama, Arkansas, Georgia, North Carolina, and Tennessee. He has provided a spiritual uplift for every place wherein he has served.

He is the editor of *Walking With God,* a Bible school curriculum for ages sixteen through adult. He is the creator and original editor for *Blueprints,* a five-year through the New Testament adult Bible school curriculum. For the past twelve years, he has hosted Call & Ask, a national question-and-answer telecast. He serves as staff editor for *Christian Echo* and *The Revivalist* Magazine and on the advisory board of Freed-Hardeman University.

He received his Bachelor's degree from Freed-Hardeman University and a Master's degree in counseling from the Theological University of America, and has done other graduate studies at University of Memphis and Southern Christian University.

He is the author of twelve books. His research paper, "Single-mothering Stimulates a Positive Family Networking Within Black

Families," was selected and presented at the Annual Graduate Research Symposium at Memphis State University.

He is married to the former Priscilla Jackson of Blytheville, Arkansas. They have four children (Terrence, Marrkus, Jondreia, and Johnathan) and five grandchildren (Kori, Brianna, Jorden, Tyler, and Destiny).

FOR MORE INFORMATION

John Marshall
P.O. Box 2136
Stone Mountain, Georgia 30086
(404) 316-5525

llahsram56@gmail.com
www.johnmarshallenterprises.com
www.solomonuniversity.org